The Assass...

JFK

— *Minute by Minute* —

JONATHAN MAYO

First published in 2013 by Short Books
an imprint of Octopus Publishing Group Ltd
Carmelite House, 50 Victoria Embankment
London, EC4Y 0DZ
www.octopusbooks.co.uk
An Hachette UK Company
www.hachette.co.uk

10 9 8 7 6 5 4 3 2 1

This paperback edition published in 2023

A CIP catalogue record for this book is available from the British Library.

ISBN 978-1-78072-627-4

Photo credits:

Cover & page 6
Copyright © Darryl Heikes photographer, *Dallas Times Herald* Collection / The Sixth
Floor Museum at Dealey Plaza

Page 10
Copyright © William Beal photographer, *Dallas Times Herald*
Collection / The Sixth Floor Museum at Dealey Plaza

Pages 18 & 268
Copyright © Tom Dillard Collection, *The Dallas Morning
News* / The Sixth Floor Museum at Dealey Plaza

Pages 138 & 238
Copyright © *Dallas Times Herald* Collection / The Sixth Floor
Museum at Dealey Plaza

Page 186
Copyright © Bill Winfrey photographer, Tom Dillard Collection,
The Dallas Morning News / The Sixth Floor Museum at Dealey Plaza

---

The extract from Alistair Cooke's 794th 'Letter from America' on page 166
is reproduced by permission of Penguin Books Ltd, and is taken from
Cooke, Alistair, *Reporting America: The Life of
the Nation 1946-2004* (Allen Lane, 2008), p.152.
Introduction and all 'Letters from America'
copyright © The Estate of Alistair Cooke, 2008.

The 'Minute by Minute' format is applied to this publication
with the permission of TBI Media

TBI ✳
The Big Idea

Printed and bound in Great Britain by Clays Ltd, Elcograf S.p.A

This FSC® label means that materials used for the product
have been responsibly sourced

MIX
Paper | Supporting
responsible forestry
FSC® C104740

For Hannah and Charlie

Contents

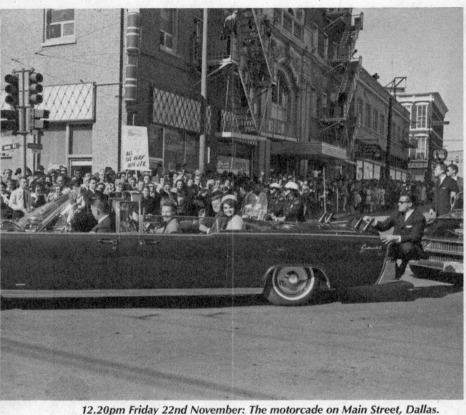

12.20pm Friday 22nd November: The motorcade on Main Street, Dallas. Agent Clint Hill is crouching on the rear step of the Lincoln.

Introduction

Half a century of conspiracy theories and endless reruns of the Zapruder footage showing President Kennedy being shot as his limousine drives through Dealey Plaza, has lessened the impact of that bizarre weekend in November 1963. You could argue that Kennedy's murder has lost its power to shock – something inconceivable to those who lived through it.

The story of what took place in Dallas is not just about President Kennedy and Lee Harvey Oswald; it's also about the scores of people who were drawn into the developing drama. Some are famous, some obscure, but it affected them all, putting them in unexpected situations, and sometimes making them behave in unexpected ways. This book is full of stories that I hope will restore the impact of the assassination.

Like Tony Zoppi, the Dallas showbiz reporter who found himself carrying the president of the United States' casket; Robert Kennedy hiding in an Army truck in the dark waiting for his brother's body to arrive on Air Force One; the pipers of the Scottish Black Watch playing at JFK's funeral covered in cuts and bruises after a bar brawl defending his name; reporter Hugh Aynesworth having to take notes on a utility bill minutes after the assassination, using a novelty pencil he bought from a small boy; six-year-old Caroline Kennedy on the way to her father's funeral, winding down the window of the limousine so she can hold Secret Service agent Bob Foster's hand as he walked alongside.

In this book I'm not interested in conspiracy theories (which all need a greater leap of faith than believing Lee Harvey Oswald and Jack Ruby were simply in the right place at the right time to do the wrong thing) and I'm not concerned much with the political background to Kennedy's presidency. I'm interested in what people are *doing* and what they are *thinking* as events unfold. In the *Minute by Minute* format, if you had a role to play, however small, you're in the book.

I love details that not only bring history to life but reveal a great deal. Jack Ruby stole a TV crew's fried chicken lunch the day before he shot Oswald (not exactly *Day of the Jackal*); a mother recognised the watch on the wrist of a reporter on TV, so she knew her son, whom she hadn't heard from in months, was okay; Lee Harvey Oswald took his wedding ring off and placed it in a china cup before he set off to assassinate Kennedy; Marina Oswald had the famous photo of her husband holding a rifle hidden in her shoe when she visited him in the police cell.

I had a treasure trove of stories and insights to plunder, thanks to contemporary accounts, numerous sworn testimonies given in the hours after the death of President Kennedy and to the 1964 Warren Commission. I owe a debt to William Manchester's book *Death of a President* (1967), and Jim Bishop's *The Day Kennedy Was Shot* (1968). Both authors interviewed many of the people involved, including Jackie and

Robert Kennedy. Where I've used dialogue, it's taken from autobiographies, police and FBI notes, or Warren Commission testimonies (remarkably, many people virtually acted out their evidence in front of the commission). The timings are based on police records, media coverage, witness statements, plus some guesswork. Events in Texas are recorded in Central Standard Time (CST), those in Washington and New York, Eastern Standard Time (EST).

12.25pm Friday 22nd November: The Presidential limousine on Main Street, Dallas.

Thursday 21st November 1963

'Welcome Mr President.'

9.00pm

At 2515 Fifth Street, Irving, Texas, 31-year-old Ruth Paine is walking into her garage. The light is already on, which is unusual. She reckons that Lee Harvey Oswald must have left it on when he was working in there earlier that evening.

Ruth is mildly irritated at his carelessness. But it can't dampen her excitement, as tomorrow the president is coming to Dallas.

11.07pm

Twenty-two minutes behind schedule, the wheels of Air Force One strike the tarmac at Carswell Air Force base on the outskirts of Fort Worth, Texas. On board is the 46-year-old President John F Kennedy and Jackie, his 34-year-old wife. He is the youngest elected leader in American history.

JFK is in Texas because he needs to win friends in the South – his support for civil rights has dented his popularity and an election is just a year away. Texas in particular needs wooing; in 1960 he beat the Republican candidate Richard Nixon here by only 46,000 votes. But Kennedy likes a challenge, and he likes even more to be away from the political intrigue of

Washington, to meet the people and win them over.

Jackie has never campaigned before and hadn't planned to be on this trip. In August, their baby son Patrick died, just a few days old; she had been expecting to be at the White House, nursing him. Many people have advised JFK not to make this trip. Dallas District Judge Sarah T Hughes told the president's aides that the journey was 'inadvisable'. Senator J William Fulbright told JFK in October, 'Dallas is a dangerous place. I wouldn't go there and don't you go!'

11.15pm

The president and his wife are walking down the steps of Air Force One, and being met by the president of the Fort Worth Chamber of Commerce, Raymond Buck. He shouts a greeting over the noise of the engines.

11.17pm

Also travelling with JFK and now leaving Air Force Two are three Democratic Texan heavyweights – the vice president Lyndon B. Johnson, the state's governor John Connally, and Senator Ralph Yarborough. Connally and Yarborough are also up for re-election in 1964 and each hopes the other will lose. They dislike each other's politics and aim to make capital out of this trip. It's got to the point where Yarborough refuses to travel in the same car as Johnson, as he's an ally of Connally.

Kennedy is sick of this damaging rift and has a plan to heal it, but the vice president is concerned that he'll only make the situation worse. Johnson, a farmer's son who left school at 15, has a very different background from the wealthy Boston upbringing of Kennedy, but they are both masterful political tacticians.

Connally, Yarborough and Johnson smile and wave to the waiting press.

11.20pm

The Kennedys are bring driven to their Fort Worth hotel in a white convertible, borrowed by the Chamber of Commerce from the golf professional Ben Hogan. The president's staff hadn't expected crowds to be out on the streets at this time of night, especially as it's raining, but the route to their hotel via the West Freeway is lined with thousands of well-wishers.

11.30pm

Thirty miles away, in Ruth Paine's Irving home, Lee Harvey Oswald's Russian wife Marina is getting into bed beside him. He's lying on his stomach with his eyes closed. Earlier they'd argued – he'd tried desperately to persuade her to leave the Paines' house where she's lodging and move back with him to Dallas, but Marina had refused. Marina was irritated because he'd turned up unexpectedly, knowing full well the agreement is he should ask Ruth's permission first.

Marina appreciates Ruth's friendship. When Marina was pregnant, Ruth had donated blood twice at Parkland Hospital to ensure that Marina qualified for free maternity care. Ruth speaks Russian, and they both have two children and both have troubled marriages. Michael Paine moved out of the house a few months ago; Lee Harvey Oswald sometimes beats Marina.

> *He always seemed like a man deeply hurt by something and I always felt somewhat like a mother to him, felt I was helping him in some way. I've always thought what a shame that something or somebody had made him the way that he was. If I had met him in the United*

States, and understood him, I probably would not have married him.

Marina Oswald interview with Hugh Aynesworth
March 1964

The Paines and the Oswalds met in March through a local Russian immigrant group. Lee doesn't like Ruth; he told Marina that she's a 'tall and stupid woman'. However, last month, just before their second child was born she did help him find a job, as a stockboy at the Texas Book Depository.

11.35pm

Waiting outside the Hotel Texas are about 2,000 people, eager to see the president and Mrs Kennedy. They shout with excitement when the car arrives. Without a word to their Secret Service agents, the couple begin shaking hands with the crowd, some of whom are holding placards with welcome messages. There are so many people in the lobby that it's chaos when the Kennedys finally walk into the hotel.

11.40pm

The Kennedys are surveying their three-room suite on the eighth floor of the Hotel Texas. The décor of Suite 850 is drab and the temperature cold, as the air conditioning has been left on full. A sign on a table says 'Check out is at 12.30pm. If you plan to stay after this time please contact the assistant manager.' The first lady's bedroom has a view of a car park and a bus station. Kenny O'Donnell, JFK's special assistant and close friend, is angry at the state of the hotel. In front of the dull brick 1920s façade is a large sign saying 'Welcome Mr President', but it doesn't feel like much of a welcome inside.

The eighth floor has been cleared of guests, except for Mrs Helen Ganss, an elderly widow for whom the Hotel Texas is home. The Secret Service is happy to let her stay. Mrs Ganss is listening to the to-ing and fro-ing in the corridor outside, and wondering if the president will ever be able to get any sleep.

11.45pm/12.45am EST

Jackie Kennedy is unpacking her clothes for the morning. They'd been chosen when the forecast for Friday had been for cold weather. The forecast now is for hot sun. Her husband calls from the next room, 'Don't get up with me. I've got to speak in that square downstairs before breakfast, so stay in bed.'

Eleven hundred miles away in the White House, their children, five-year-old Caroline and two-year-old John Jr are fast asleep. Earlier Caroline had been to a friend's party, and John to a toyshop with Secret Service agent Tom Wells. Their 61-year-old English nanny, Maud Shaw, is asleep in her quarters between the children's rooms, after an evening spent knitting. Downstairs, West Wing staff are making their way home after a preview of *From Russia With Love* in the White House cinema.

Peter Saccu, the catering manager for the Hotel Texas, has arrived to sort out the air conditioning in the president's suite. Kennedy asks if a window in his bedroom could be opened slightly. Saccu warns him that the noise of the freight trains in the nearby sidings might keep him awake, but the president smiles and says that won't bother him.

11.55pm

Kennedy bodyguard and general dogsbody John 'Muggsy' O'Leary is standing at the entrance to the hotel. He spots a man lying on the roof of a building across the road, level with the presidential suite. He sends up a policeman to catch him.

The midnight to 8am shift of Secret Service agents is taking over the watch outside Suite 850.

11.55am Friday 22nd November: The Presidential limousine leaves Love Field Airport, Dallas.

Friday 22nd November 1963

'We're heading into nut country today...'

00.10am

Reporter Roy Stamps is in the hotel lobby looking for a cup of coffee. He's in the middle of setting up his radio equipment in the car park across from the hotel, ready for the president's early morning speech to the public. He bumps into a group of Secret Service agents who've just finished their shift, and are looking for a place to eat. Stamps suggests they all head to the Fort Worth Press Club.

1.30am

Richard Nixon, whom Kennedy narrowly defeated in the 1960 presidential election, is asleep in the Baker Hotel in Dallas. He has a successful law practice and one of his clients is Pepsi Cola, so he's in town for a bottlers' convention across the street from the Trade Mart, where JFK is due to give a speech later that day. The 35th, and the future 36th and 37th presidents of the United States are all asleep, a few miles from each other.

1.45am

Nine Secret Service agents, unwinding after their shift, are drinking in the Fort Worth Press Club with Malcolm 'Mac' Kilduff, the president's acting press secretary. It normally closes at midnight, but the club is making an exception for the White House party.

Lee Harvey Oswald isn't asleep. Marina is resting her foot on her husband's leg. He roughly shakes her off.

'My, he's in a mean mood,' Marina thinks.

3.00am

Seven of the Secret Service agents, despite the fact most of them have to ride in the presidential motorcade in Dallas later that morning, have moved on from the Press Club and are now in the Cellar Coffee House five minutes away. As they arrive, they introduce themselves to the manager Dick Mackie and order 'Salty Dicks' – a nonalcoholic speciality of the club.

5.05am

The Secret Service agents leave the Cellar Coffee House and head for their cars.

6.00am

Outside the Hotel Texas, a crowd is already beginning to gather in the rain, eager to get a good place for the president's speech. They watch the presidential seal being fixed to the flatbed truck he'll be speaking from. Policemen in raincoats watch the crowd from the top of nearby buildings.

6.30am

The Oswalds' alarm is going off, but Lee doesn't stir. Marina is already awake.

In the pressroom set up in the Hotel Texas, the White House reporters are sitting by their typewriters eating breakfast and reading advance copies of the president's Trade Mart speech.

'There will always be dissident voices raised... but today other voices are heard in the land... voices preaching doctrines wholly unrelated to reality, wholly unrelated to the Sixties, doctrines which apparently assure that words will suffice without weapons... and that peace is a sign of weakness...'

NBC correspondent Robert MacNeil has always been sceptical about Kennedy, but he's impressed by the speech and looks forward to hearing the president deliver it. It's MacNeil's first presidential trip.

6.40am

Having waited ten minutes for her husband to stir, Marina says, 'Time to get up.'

Oswald gets up, washes and changes into his work shirt and grey trousers.

'Have you bought those shoes you were going to get?' he asks.

'No, I haven't had time.'

'You must get those shoes, Mama. And don't get up, I'll get breakfast myself.'

7.18am

Oswald kisses their children, one-month-old Rachel and

two-year-old June, who are both still asleep, but he doesn't kiss Marina. He's just about to leave the bedroom when he turns and says, 'I've left some money on the bureau. Take it and buy everything you and Junie and Rachel need. Bye-bye.'

Once out of the bedroom Oswald takes off his wedding ring and puts it in a little china cup that belonged to Marina's grandmother. He's never taken the ring off before. He then leaves $187 in bills on the dresser, almost all the money he has, and quietly walks out of the house towards the garage.

By the age of ten, Lee Harvey Oswald had lived in 13 different homes and attended six different schools. He was violent and aggressive and social workers described him as 'an emotionally-starved, affectionless youngster'. His father died before he was born and his mother Marguerite was so controlling that his two half-brothers joined the Marines to escape her. In 1956, a week after turning 17, Lee did the same.

But the Marines didn't take to the recruit whom they saw as an eccentric troublemaker, with a growing interest in communism, and so happily gave him an early discharge. In 1959 Oswald defected to the Soviet Union where he met and married 19-year-old Marina Nikolaevna Prusakova. The Soviet dream, like the Marines, didn't work out and within two years he was back in the United States. Recently he's been more interested in supporting Fidel Castro's Cuba than holding down a steady job.

Oswald is leaving the Paines' garage and heading down the street carrying a rifle wrapped up in brown paper.

7.20am

When Oswald stays with Marina, a neighbour of the Paines' 18-year-old Wesley Frazier, who also works at the Book Depository, gives him a lift. Oswald's heading to Frazier's house, something he's never done before. Frazier's sister Linnie Mae is in her kitchen watching him.

> *I saw him as he crossed the street and come across my driveway to where Wesley had his car parked by the carport... He was carrying a package in a sort of a heavy brown bag, heavier than a grocery bag it looked to me... He carried it in his right hand, had the top sort of folded down and it almost touched the ground as he carried it... He opened the right back door and I just saw that he was laying the package down so I closed the door. I didn't recognise him as he walked across my carport and at that moment I wondered who was fixing to come to my back door...*
>
> **Linnie Mae Randle testimony to the Warren Commission**
> **11th March 1964**

7.22am

It's raining as Wesley Frazier and Oswald pull out of the carport.

'What's the package, Lee?'

'Curtain rods.'

Frazier asks if he had fun playing with his children last night, and Oswald laughs and said he did. His children are one of the few things Frazier can get him to talk about. Even though they've been working together for a month, Frazier doesn't even know his surname. He puts his foot on the accelerator as they're running late – they need to be at work by 8am.

7.30am

George Thomas, the president's valet, is knocking on the door of the master bedroom of Suite 850.

'Mr President, it's raining out.' He hears his boss stir and reply, 'That's too bad' and then groan.

The rain is posing a problem that it's Kenny O'Donnell's job to fix. O'Donnell is an old college friend of Jack's brother Robert; his official role is appointments secretary, but like JFK's other close aides he works on anything and everything. O'Donnell is known as 'The Cobra' because of his piercing stare; Jackie calls him 'The Wolfhound' because of his relentless dedication to her husband. No one gets to see JFK without getting O'Donnell's approval first.

He has to decide soon if the presidential limousine in Dallas should have its bubbletop on or off. If it's on, then the crowds won't get a good look at JFK and Jackie, but if he leaves it off and it rains, the president and his wife won't be best pleased. He ponders this as looks out at the rain from his hotel room window.

Admiral Dr George Burkley, the president's physician, puts his head round his hotel room door and looks towards Suite 850. The Secret Service detail nod their heads, letting him know that all is well.

7.40am

Kennedy has showered and is beginning a routine essential for what will be a punishing day. After making two speeches this morning in Fort Worth, he'll fly to Dallas, and after a motorcade through the city make a speech at the Trade Mart. Then he'll fly to Austin for more official functions, before heading to the vice president's ranch for a rest.

JFK sits down, attaches a large back brace round his middle and ties its laces tightly. He then slips large stretchable bandages up over his hips to support the bottom of his torso. Since he was a teenager he has suffered from a chronic bad back, which means for much of the time he's in pain. Sometimes it's so bad he uses crutches or a walking stick – but never in public.

It's a condition that was made worse in August 1943 when motor torpedo boat PT-109, under his command, was rammed by a Japanese destroyer, and he was flung onto the deck. Kennedy's dramatic rescue of his crew turned him into a war hero.

Thirty-two-year-old Clint Hill, the first lady's ex-Army Secret Service bodyguard, has arrived outside Suite 850 and is being told that he's not needed for a while, as Mrs Kennedy won't be leaving her room for another hour. Hill gets himself a coffee and a roll.

7.45am

The president, now dressed in a blue pinstripe suit with a blue silk tie, is looking down from his wife's window at the people in the car park.

'Look at that crowd! Just look – isn't that terrific?'

He then heads to his room to get some breakfast.

7.56am

Wesley Frazier and Lee Harvey Oswald have arrived at a car park close to the Book Depository. Frazier gets out of his car but Oswald is already striding on ahead, with his package held vertically against his body. Frazier thinks it's strange, as they normally always walk into work together. By the time he gets to the back door Oswald has disappeared. The Hertz Rent-a-Car clock on the top of the building says 7.56.

Waiter George Jackson, who has just brought breakfast to Suite 850, asks valet George Thomas a favour – would he be happy to ask the president for a souvenir? Thomas agrees and steps into the room and whispers in Kennedy's ear. JFK immediately gets up, goes out to Jackson, shakes him by the hand and gives him a PT-109 tie clip – a small silver torpedo boat with 'Kennedy' on the full length of the hull.

8.30am

Kennedy is shouting down the phone to Kenny O'Donnell. He's just seen the morning's newspapers and they are yet again featuring the rivalry between Yarborough, Connally and Johnson. The *Dallas Morning News* has on its front page: 'Yarborough Snubs LBJ', referring to arguments about who rides in what car in the motorcades. Kennedy wants O'Donnell to tell Yarborough in no uncertain terms that he has a choice: ride with Johnson today – or walk.

8.43am

Without a hat or a raincoat, the president, his hair still wet from the hotel shower, is making his way across Eighth Street. Walking behind him are Congressman Jim Wright, Senator Yarborough, Governor Connally and a sour-looking Vice President Johnson. NBC reporter Robert MacNeil, watching in the crowd, thinks that they look like naughty schoolboys.

Johnson is nervous about how Texans view him. He knows many Southerners had expected him to curb what they saw as Kennedy's dangerous liberal views. In fact, LBJ has been side-lined by Kennedy and surprised the South by speaking out in favour of civil rights.

In 1960, Johnson, campaigning in his 'LBJ Special' train, had won the South for Kennedy. He directly confronted Southern Baptist suspicions about Kennedy's Catholicism: their doubts about whether his ultimate allegiance was to the USA or the Vatican. Johnson told them how JFK had loved his older brother Joe, a pilot killed in the Second World War.

'When he took off that morning on his dangerous mission,' Johnson would tell the crowds, his voice almost breaking, 'nobody asked him what church he went to. After he went down in a burning plane over the English Channel so that we could have free speech and live as free men, not a soul got up in a pulpit and asked what church he went to.' At each stop, Johnson's audience listened in absolute silence.

8.45am

Jim Wright tells the crowd that this is the 'proudest day in the history of Fort Worth'. To great applause, the president walks up to the microphone.

'There are no faint hearts in Fort Worth and I appreciate your being here this morning. Mrs Kennedy is organising herself. It takes longer.' This is greeted by a wolf whistle.

'But of course she looks better than we do when she does so.' The crowd laughs and cheers.

Jackie can hear him over the PA as she sits at her dressing table. She's happy that it's raining as that means the bubbletop will be on the limousine and it'll keep her hair from blowing about.

She's never found being the president's wife easy. Three years earlier, when asked by Angier Duke, the White House chief of protocol, what she might like to do as first lady she replied, 'As little as possible. I'm a mother. I'm a wife. I'm not a public official.'

Down below, Kennedy is praising Fort Worth's aviation industry for its contribution to the defence of America and to the space race, which, he says, America is now winning.

8.55am

The radio audience listening on local station WBAP can hear women squeal as the president steps off the podium and starts to shake hands with the crowd.

'We have a long microphone about 14 inches long which is like a long pistol. A Secret Service agent just approached us and said, "Just don't put that in front of the president",' WBAP reporter David Daniel says.

The crowd is shouting to the president, 'Come over here! Come over here!'

Kennedy is passing Robert MacNeil and they look at each other. MacNeil thinks that his eyes look cold.

As he passes Henry Brandon of *The Sunday Times*, whom he knows well, and the only foreign correspondent on the trip, JFK mutters, 'We're doing better than we thought.'

8.57am

The president is walking into the hotel lobby wiping his right hand with a handkerchief, making it dirty. A woman calls out that he hasn't shaken her hand so Congressman Jim Wright takes it in his and stretches out with his other hand to touch the president. She's delighted with that.

9.05am

Local station KRLD-TV is about to take live coverage of the president's Breakfast Speech in the hotel's Grand Ballroom. At the moment they're showing viewers shots of 2,000 excited guests, invited by the Fort Worth Chamber of Commerce. KRLD-TV commentator Mike Wallace has a good position in the ballroom, looking into the kitchen from where the president will enter.

Wallace is filling for time and he's reaching for some prepared notes. JFK's handshakes with the people outside prompt him to talk about how difficult crowds can be for the Secret Service. He describes the last assassination of a president – the shooting of William McKinley by anarchist Leon Czolgosz in 1901.

'As in many important occasions in the history of the world no one seemed to sense that anything different was going to happen. The assassin shattered that picture quickly.'

His sombre commentary is at odds with the pictures of the happy, expectant crowd.

Secret Service agent Clint Hill, who has been responsible for the first lady's protection for the last three years, is patiently waiting as she buttons her white gloves. She's wearing a two-piece rose-pink Chanel suit with a navy blouse and he thinks that she looks lovely, but Hill's anxious as she's needed at the breakfast. Jackie reckons Hill is the sharpest of the White House detail, a perfectionist like her husband, and 'one of us'.

'I hope you slept well,' she says to him.

'We've got another long day ahead, Mrs Kennedy.'

'I never realised how tiring campaigning could be.'

'Did you know that the president is waiting for you at breakfast?'

'I wasn't planning on going to the breakfast.'

'I know, Mrs Kennedy, but the president wants you down there – right now.'

Jackie looks in the mirror.

'Okay, I just need to put on my hat.'

She reaches for a pink pillbox hat on the dressing table.

9.10am

Outside the ballroom, the president runs into Yarborough and tells him he must ride in the car with Johnson.

'For Christ's sake cut it out, Ralph!'

The senator protests that he rode with Johnson from the airport the night before. Kennedy points out it was in the dark, and it's not enough. He heads for the ballroom.

9.25am

Jackie Kennedy is standing with Clint Hill in the kitchen of the Hotel Texas, waiting for toastmaster Raymond Buck to finish his lengthy welcome speech. The kitchen staff stare at her. JFK took his place on the top table 15 minutes earlier.

Finally Buck announces, 'And now is an event I know you have all been waiting for!'

As the first lady walks through the tables, the cheers are louder than for the president. Some people are standing on their chairs to see her. On the top table, John Connally's wife Nellie is mortified – she's also wearing a pink wool suit.

At the back of the room, Kennedy's Air Force aide Godfrey McHugh is saying to NBC's Robert MacNeil with a big grin, 'What kind of an entrance do you call that?'

'Tactical,' MacNeil replies.

Jackie takes her seat, and Clint Hill follows, scanning the faces in the room.

The president starts to speak.

'Two years ago, I introduced myself in Paris by saying that I was the man who had accompanied Mrs Kennedy to Paris. I am getting somewhat that same sensation as I travel around Texas. Nobody wonders what Lyndon and I wear...'

The audience roars with laughter.

> *Sometimes he was a little bit sick... and sometimes I didn't know – he want to be popular, so everyone know who is Lee Harvey Oswald.*
>
> *Marina Oswald testimony to the Warren Commission 24th July 1964*

9.35am

In the Texas Book Depository, Lee Harvey Oswald is standing by one of the windows on the first floor. It's an old building, stranded in a new development called Dealey Plaza. Its floorboards have sunken paths, worn down by hundreds of feet over the decades.

Oswald's job is to pick up orders for schoolbooks, find the books and then take them to the first-floor shipping desk. He asks colleague James 'Junior' Jarman why there are people gathering outside on the front steps. Jarman tells him it's because the presidential motorcade will pass by. 'Do you know which way he's coming?' Oswald asks. Jarman explains that the route will take the president right past their building.

'Oh, I see,' says Oswald and goes back to filling orders.

Mac Kilduff, the president's acting press secretary, is looking through the *Dallas Morning News*. He sees something that makes him go pale.

9.45am

In downtown Dallas, WFAA radio reporter Travis Linn is asking his colleague AJ L'Hoste to set up a portable tape recorder in Dealey Plaza, to capture the sound of the president's motorcade going by, for a piece for broadcast later in the day. Linn has to be at the Trade Mart so can't do it himself. He asks L'Hoste to place it on the corner of Houston and Elm, opposite the depository building.

9.55am

Kenny O'Donnell comes into Suite 850 as the president says to Jackie, 'How about California in two weeks?'

She smiles.

'Sure, I'll be there.'

O'Donnell, who knows that Jackie is a vote winner, grins so broadly that she bursts out laughing. Rarely does the Cobra smile.

10.14am

Kennedy is on the phone wishing former vice president John Nance Garner a happy 95th birthday. Serving under the dynamic Franklin D Roosevelt in the 1930s, he'd not had much to do, and consequently called the vice presidential post 'not worth a bucket of warm piss'.

Jackie is walking through the suite and noticing for the first time that the walls are covered with original paintings by Monet, Van Gogh and Picasso, put there just for them. When her husband has finished talking to John Nance Garner, she suggests they call whomever is responsible for the kind gesture.

Roy Kellerman, the Secret Service agent in charge of this trip, needs a decision about the bubbletop. He calls Kenny O'Donnell who says, 'If the weather is clear and it's not raining, have that bubbletop off.'

10.18am

The phone rings in the home of Ruth Carter Johnson, the wife of a Fort Worth newspaper executive. She's just been watching the president's speech on the television and is stunned to hear his voice on the end of the line. He apologises for not calling earlier and thanks her for the paintings.

It will be the president's last telephone call.

10.20am

O'Donnell is breaking the relaxed mood, by showing the president and first lady what Mac Kilduff found in the *Dallas Morning News*. It's a full-page advertisement headlined 'WELCOME MR KENNEDY TO DALLAS' and it accuses him of being soft on communism, while allowing his brother Robert to 'prosecute loyal Americans'. It's signed 'The American Fact-Finding Committee, Bernard Weissman, Chairman'. It has a black border as if it were a death announcement.

JFK looks at Jackie.

'We're heading into nut country today. You know, last night would have been a hell of a night to assassinate a president. There was the rain, and the night, and we were all getting jostled. Suppose a man had a pistol in a briefcase...'

The president points his index finger at the wall and jerks his thumb twice imitating a gun, '... and then melted away in the crowd.'

In October, JFK had invited the writer Jim Bishop to the White House, and they'd talked about his book *The Day Lincoln Was Shot*.

'My feelings about assassinations are identical with Mr Lincoln's. Anyone who wants to exchange his life for mine can take it. They just can't protect that much.'

10.30am

For the trip to Dallas, Kennedy is changing into a lightweight grey and blue suit with a blue striped shirt and blue silk tie.

10.40am

Hugh Aynesworth is the science reporter for the *Dallas Morning News* and is sitting in the paper's cafeteria. He's looking at the black-bordered advertisement and thinking it's the most outrageous thing he's seen in a Dallas paper. Aynesworth looks up and sees strip club owner Jack Ruby queuing up for breakfast, probably hoping to collar nightclub columnist Tony Zoppi to persuade him to use a photo of one of his girls in the paper.

Aynesworth thinks Ruby is an obnoxious hustler, always promoting some useless product, and ingratiating himself with the police. Ruby has a hair-trigger temper – he's seen him chuck a drunk down the stairs of one of his clubs and then proceed to kick him as he tried to stumble away. Aynesworth watches as Ruby first takes a seat and then cuts a hole in his newspaper so that he can spy on the cashier who's wearing a short skirt.

10.50am

Fifty-eight-year-old Dallas dressmaker Abraham Zapruder is driving home to collect his 8mm Bell & Howell movie camera. He'd meant to bring it into work that morning and his secretary persuaded him to go back and get it.

'How many times will you have a crack at colour movies of the president?'

11.00am

The motorcade is pulling away from the Hotel Texas, heading for Main Street, and then Carswell Air Force base. Yarborough is reluctantly travelling in the same car as the vice president.

Richard Nixon is on American Airlines Flight 82 out of Dallas, heading home to New York.

A man sitting next to him on the plane says, 'But for want of a few thousand votes here and there, that might have been you heading into Dallas today.'

'I try not to think about things like that,' Nixon replies.

11.23am

President and Mrs Kennedy are climbing the steps of Air Force One and waving to the crowd. Its pilot, Colonel Jim Swindal, is looking at his watch. They're behind schedule. On board, Mac Kilduff is thinking of the day ahead.

'I'll be glad when this next stop is over. It's the only one that worries me,' he says to no one in particular.

11.30am

On the chartered Pan Am 707 carrying 40 members of the press from Fort Worth to Dallas, is Harry Brandon of *The Sunday Times*. He's here because he's been told that there might be trouble in Dallas. Brandon is putting a blank sheet of paper in his portable typewriter and hammering out his piece.

'I crossed the American border by jet yesterday into hostile Texas with a small guerilla band of White House officials, led by President Kennedy. As his secret weapon and perhaps also with his security in mind he had brought Mrs Kennedy along...'

11.38am

After a 13-minute flight from Fort Worth, the president's Boeing 707 is landing at Love Field. They could have driven to Dallas, but as O'Donnell had said to the team who planned the trip, 'It's good logistics but poor politics' – the president would miss out on a striking airport arrival photo opportunity and an impressive motorcade through the city.

Behind the airport's wire fence, there's a large crowd to see President and Mrs Kennedy. JFK sees them through the window and says to Kenny O'Donnell, 'The trip is turning out to be terrific. Here we are in Dallas, and it looks like everything in Texas is going to be fine for us.'

But not all the crowd is there to cheer. Alongside placards saying, 'WE LOVE JACK' are others saying, 'YOUR A TRAITER' (sic) and less concisely, 'MR PRESIDENT, BECAUSE OF YOUR SOCIALIST TENDENCIES AND BECAUSE OF YOUR SURRENDER TO COMMUNISM I HOLD YOU IN COMPLETE CONTEMPT.'

WFAA–TV commentator Jay Watson sees that the 1961 Lincoln armour-plated presidential limousine that'll take Kennedy through Dallas, has its top down.

'Evidently for all of you people who will see the parade downtown you will see a glimpse of the president and the first lady in the flesh rather than through a bubbletop glass,' he says.

11.42am

From the rear door of the 707, Jackie steps into the Texas heat, her pink suit vivid in the sun. Her husband follows her. WFAA-TV's Jay Watson, broadcasting live, says with a touch of sarcasm, 'I can see his suntan all the way from here!'

JFK turns slightly as he walks down the steps to ease his back pain.

As the Secret Service men pour out of the front door of the aircraft, down the steps and towards the rear, Jackie is given a bouquet of red roses by Dearie Cabell, the wife of the mayor of Dallas.

11.44am

Shadowed by the experienced Roy Kellerman, who has served three other presidents, Kennedy is at the fence talking and shaking hands with the crowd. Ronnie Dugger, the editor of the *Texas Observer*, is scribbling in his notebook, 'Kennedy is showing that he is not afraid.'

Jackie is trying to stay as close to her husband as possible. Someone in the crowd snatches the head of one of her roses as a souvenir.

Out in Irving, Marina Oswald is watching the television

coverage as Rachel runs around in her pyjamas. Marina had woken up feeling down, but this is really cheering her up.

11.47am

Bill Greer, the president's driver, has brought the midnight-blue Lincoln to within a few feet of him. Standing up in the jump seats behind Greer is Governor Connally, wearing a ten-gallon hat and a big smile. Nellie Connally takes the jump seat next to her husband. Kennedy helps his wife, who's shielding her eyes from the bright sun, into the back of the car. Roy Kellerman notices the president wince slightly as he gets in.

11.54am

Charlie Givens, one of the dozen stockboys in the Texas Book Depository, is walking across the sixth floor. He's looking for his jacket with his cigarettes in its pocket. He thinks he's alone, so jumps when Lee Harvey Oswald walks towards him carrying a clipboard. They only ever speak when Oswald makes a mistake filling out order forms.

'Boy, are you going downstairs? It's near lunchtime.'

'No, sir, and when you get downstairs, close the elevator gate,' Oswald replies.

The elevator is automatic and works only if the gate is closed. Charlie Givens takes it downstairs. The next time he sees Oswald will be on the television news.

Marina Oswald is still in her nightclothes, watching the motorcade on WFAA-TV, and enjoying every minute of the coverage, even though her English isn't good enough to understand what the commentators are saying. Ruth Paine is in the kitchen of the little ranch house preparing lunch.

'You certainly can't say that the people of Dallas haven't given you a nice welcome...'

11.55am

The motorcade is pulling away at the start of its ten-mile journey to the Trade Mart.

'Lancer and Lace departing,' Roy Kellerman is saying into his radio, using the codewords for the Kennedys.

The lead car in front of the president is a white unmarked police sedan, driven by Dallas Police chief Jesse Curry, and containing Secret Service agents and County Sheriff Bill Decker. Curry has deployed 700 policemen, Texas Rangers and firefighters to keep order. In October, Adlai Stevenson, the US ambassador to the United Nations, had been spat on and struck with a placard by a right-wing crowd, as he walked in Dallas. The police had lost control and Curry was determined his force would not be embarrassed again.

In a television broadcast on Wednesday night he'd declared, 'Nothing must occur that is disrespectful or degrading to the president of the United States...We will take immediate action if any suspicious conduct is observed.'

The son of a policeman, Jesse Curry has been in the force for 27 years, the last four as chief. He is hard-working and constantly aware that the city fathers look to him to protect Dallas's image.

Behind the president's limousine, at a regulation distance of five feet, is a Secret Service car, so large it's nicknamed the 'Queen Mary'. It carries eight agents, including Clint Hill. They are all armed. Riding with them is Kenny O'Donnell and the president's other advisor Dave Powers, part of the so-called Irish Mafia, who has known JFK since his first campaign for the

Senate in 1946. Powers is famous for his lack of pretension and informality – he once said to the Shah of Iran, 'I want you to know that you're my kind of Shah...' Powers has a cine camera with him, and every now and then he stands up and films a few seconds of the president's limo in front.

The rest of the motorcade consists of the vice president's car, a press car with a radiophone, camera cars, press buses, a sedan carrying Admiral Burkley, the president's doctor (who is unhappy about being so far away from the president), a car with a White House Signal Corps officer, police cars and motorcycle escorts. It stretches for half a mile.

The Secret Service is concerned about the motorcade, as the Boss, as they call him, had half-jokingly asked one of their supervisors four days earlier to 'keep the Ivy League charlatans off the back of the car' (a reference to their youth and sharp suits). He doesn't want the agents blocking his view of the crowd. Clint Hill is on the running board of the car behind, and feeling too far away.

The Secret Service is very aware of the risk of assassination. Formed in the aftermath of the murder of President Lincoln, on the walls of their office in the White House are prints and engravings of the killings of presidents, as well as the weapons and bullets that killed them. To keep the president alive is their only function.

At every intersection of the route are a reporter and photographer from the *Dallas Times Herald*. The paper's news editor Charles F Dameron has planned the day with military precision because he fears that some 'nut will do something stupid'. If something does happen, the *Times Herald* will have it covered.

11.57am

The president's motorcade is making its way through the outskirts of Dallas. Jackie has her sunglasses on because of the blinding noonday sun; the temperature is now in the mid-70s. The president asks her to take them off, as they'll make her look aloof. Over the past three years he has had plenty of sunglasses stolen from his jacket pocket as souvenirs; Admiral Burkley has some spares in his doctor's bag. Jackie puts her glasses on her lap, but every now and then quickly puts them on when the road looks deserted. Between herself and her husband she's put the bouquet of red roses.

12.08am

Robert MacNeil's press car is passing a sign that says, 'I HOLD YOU JFK AND YOUR BLIND SOCIALISM IN COMPLETE CONTEMPT'.

12.09am

Kennedy calls out to Bill Greer to stop. It takes Police chief Jesse Curry in the car in front a moment to notice – his car swiftly reverses. The president has seen a group of children with a large hand-written sign saying, 'MR PRESIDENT, PLEASE STOP AND SHAKE OUR HANDS. OUR NEIGHBORS SAID YOU WOULDN'T'. His car is soon surrounded by screaming children, and Roy Kellerman and the other Secret Service agents struggle to keep order. They've been unhappy for a long time that the president resists their attempts to keep crowds away from him.

A woman shouts, 'It worked! Our sign worked!'

12.12pm

Two of Oswald's colleagues – Harold Norman and Junior Jarman – are on the fifth floor of the Book Depository, which gives them a great view of Dealey Plaza. They're joined by Bonnie Ray Williams who's just finished his lunch. He was up on the sixth floor but it was so quiet he thought he'd watch the motorcade with his friends.

12.16pm

On Harwood Street a crowd is surging towards the president's car. Bill Greer has to slow down to a crawl, forcing the police motorcyclist on Jackie's side to drop back. Clint Hill runs forward to cover her; he knows that despite her outward calm, she hates crowds. People are hanging out of the windows cheering and waving – the sidewalks are four deep in places.

12.17pm

Dave Powers puts down his cine camera, as he's run out of film.

> *I noticed on the sixth floor of the building that there was a man back from the window... he was standing and holding a rifle. This appeared to me to be a fairly high-powered rifle because of the scope and the relative proportion of the scope to the rifle... and we thought momentarily that maybe we should tell someone...*
>
> **Arnold Rowland testimony to the Warren Commission**
> **10th March 1964**

12.20pm

The motorcade has turned onto Main Street, and Bill Greer is forced to drive on the left-hand side of the road to keep the president (who is on the right of the car) away from the crowds spilling off the sidewalks. Once again, the motorcycle escort on the left has to drop back as there is no longer room between the president's limousine and the crowd. Clint Hill ignores the Boss's order and gets on the rear step of the car, holds onto the handrail and crouches as low as he can. He's concerned that someone might try and grab Jackie or throw something into the car.

In the car behind the president, his special assistant Kenny O'Donnell is on his feet, delighted.

'There's certainly nothing wrong with this crowd,' he says to Dave Powers.

O'Donnell's particularly pleased to see that Jackie has followed his advice and is staying turned to her side of the street, so that everyone gets a glimpse of at least one of the couple. Mac Kilduff, who had worried about this part of the trip most of all, is also feeling that he's misjudged the people of Dallas.

Lady Bird Johnson looks up and sees Mary Griffith, an old friend who does dress alterations for her, waving from a department store window. She smiles and waves back.

12.21pm

Alone on the sixth floor of the depository, directly above Harold Norman and Bonnie Ray Williams, Oswald is moving some boxes to the south-east corner close to a window with an unobstructed view of the route. He arranges some behind him so he's hidden from view in case anyone else comes in. Oswald then places a box by the window on which to rest his Italian Second World War Mannlicher-Carcano rifle. In the Marine Corps all his best shooting scores were with a braced rifle.

He only has four bullets – all left over from his last practice session.

Arnold Rowland and his wife Barbara are standing opposite the Book Depository. Something catches Arnold's eye on the sixth floor. He can see a man at the window holding a gun, what looks like a fairly high-powered rifle because it has a scope. One of the man's hands is at the gunstock, just above the trigger, the other on the barrel. Arnold and Barbara discuss whether they should tell the policeman standing 12 feet away from them, but they reckon the man at the window must be a Secret Service agent. They'd seen them positioned like that in the movies.

Howard Brennan, a 44-year-old steamfitter who has just finished his lunch at a nearby café, is looking at the man too, and thinking that he looks in his own little world.

12.22pm

A teenage boy is running alongside the president's motorcade shouting, 'Slow down! Slow down!' He starts to take a picture but is bundled into the crowd by agent Jack Ready, knocking a number of people over.

12.23pm

Lyndon Johnson is sullen. He's so far back from the president, the cheers have died down by the time he passes. Most people aren't looking at him, but up the street towards the disappearing president and first lady.

Senator Yarborough, riding with Johnson, is looking uneasily at the people watching from the windows on Main Street. Although the sidewalks are full of Kennedy fans, above them, the faces are hard and unimpressed.

12.25pm

Halfway down Main Street, Dallas FBI special agent James Hosty, who monitors right-wing groups in the city, is watching the motorcade pass by. A keen Kennedy supporter (rare in the Dallas FBI), he's shocked at how unprotected the president is; apart from Clint Hill, all the Secret Service agents are in the car behind. He then crosses the street and goes into the Oriental Café to get himself some lunch.

Sitting in front of Jackie Kennedy, Nellie Connally is listening to the president saying, 'Thank you, thank you, thank you.' She wonders why he bothers, when no one can hear him. Whenever Jackie waves her white-gloved hand, the crowd goes wild. Nellie, a proud Texan, is thinking she feels just like a mother whose children are performing in front of the relatives exactly as she'd hoped.

Senator Yarborough is finding this part of town increasingly oppressive. He can't wait to get President Kennedy out of here.

As the crowds are thinner as they near the end of Main Street, Clint Hill jumps off the back of the president's Lincoln and heads to the follow-up car.

12.26pm

Abraham Zapruder is clutching his 8mm Bell & Howell home

movie camera. He's standing on a concrete block about four feet off the ground and he's got a good view of the street. He just hopes he doesn't get dizzy and fall over looking down the telescopic lens.

John Stemmons and Trammell Crow, co-owners of the Trade Mart, are asking a Secret Service agent the correct way to greet the president of the United States and the first lady.

12.28pm

Bob Edwards and Ronald Fischer are on their lunch break, and standing on the edge of the kerb. Bob punches Ronald on the shoulder.

'Look at that guy there in that window. He looks like he's hiding from someone amongst those boxes!'

They watch the man, who's standing transfixed, gaze down towards the end of Elm Street.

On top of a concrete column close to Ronald Fischer, the dial of a portable tape recorder flickers, showing it's picking up the sound of the excited crowd.

12.29pm

Fifteen-year-old Amos Euins got permission from his school to come and see the president. He's on a street corner with no one else around him. He's waving to the president and the president is waving back.

Oswald gets in position behind a partially open window.

12.30pm

Jackie Kennedy is now really feeling the heat of the midday sun. She can see an underpass up ahead and thinks that it'll be cool when they drive beneath it.

Nellie Connally is turning to President Kennedy. 'You certainly can't say that the people of Dallas haven't given you a nice welcome.'

'No, you certainly can't,' he replies.

Chief Curry in the lead car is easily making the turn into Elm Street, but for Bill Greer in the 21-foot Lincoln it's harder. The car almost stops.

Bonnie Ray Williams sees JFK brush his hair back from his face. Abraham Zapruder starts filming.

Agent Rufus Youngblood in Johnson's car is looking at the time on the Hertz clock on top of the depository building – it says 12.30. They are only five minutes late for the Trade Mart luncheon.

Clint Hill notices some open windows in the depository, but then there have been plenty of open windows during the drive through Dallas.

A large woman in a pink dress is shouting delightedly, 'She's got my dress on! She's got my dress on!'

Charles Brendt holds his son up to see the president.

Reporter Mary Woodward can't believe that she's actually going to see Jackie Kennedy.

'Please look this way!'

The car starts to move downhill, away from the Book Depository.

Looking through his telescopic sight 190 feet away, Lee Harvey Oswald sees the president's limousine emerge from behind a tree. He squeezes the trigger of his mail order rifle. The president is waving. The bullet leaves the barrel at 1700 feet per second.

The dial on reporter Travis Linn's tape machine flickers as it picks up the sound of a gunshot echoing round the plaza. Many in the crowd think it's a firecracker; Jackie thinks it's a car that's backfired.

Virgie Rachley, watching on the street, is surprised to see sparks fly off the pavement behind the president's limousine. A splinter of concrete hits car salesman James Tague in the cheek. Oswald has missed his target.

Policeman Marrion Baker is riding his motorbike about 20 yards behind the president's car and recognises the noise of a high-powered rifle. He looks up and sees pigeons flying off the roof of the Book Depository. He's now accelerating towards the building...

Twenty-year-old James Worrell Jr has his back to the depository and is looking straight up. He can see a gun barrel sticking out of a window.

Oswald fires again.

The second bullet hits the president in the back, passing

through his throat and hitting Governor Connally, going through his chest and shattering a rib. Now travelling backwards, the bullet hits his wrist and ends up embedded in his left thigh. Connally looks down at the blood pouring from his chest.

'My God! They are going to kill us all!'

He thinks he's been fatally hit and slumps towards Nellie. Kennedy doesn't fall – his back brace keeps him upright and an easy target.

Jackie looks at Connally and then turns to her husband who has a quizzical look on his face.

On Air Force One the pilot Colonel James Swindal is on the Secret Service radio frequency. He can hear Ray Kellerman in the front of the president's car shout, '*Dagger* cover *Volunteer*!' the codewords for the agent Rufus Youngblood and the vice president. Youngblood has already shoved Johnson down into his seat and is lying on top of him to shield him, his knees in his back. Yarborough doesn't duck too far down, as he doesn't want to look a coward in front of all these Texans. He can smell gunpowder.

In the depository building, Bonnie Ray Williams heard the second shot rattle the windows and he's now being showered in dust from the wooden ceiling. Next to him, Harold Norman says, 'I can even hear the shell being ejected from the gun hitting the floor.'

In the car behind the president, Secret Service agent Glen Bennett sees him shot in the right shoulder.

'He's hit!'

Bennett reaches for the assault rifle hidden on the floor of the car but colleague George Hickey, in his first presidential motorcade, has already grabbed it, so he pulls out his revolver looking desperately for the gunman.

Schoolboy Amos Euins is staring at what looks like a pipe sticking out of the sixth-floor window. He can see a man holding it...

The plaza echoes with the sound of people screaming.

Clint Hill is sprinting towards the Kennedys' car to shield them, the only agent to so do. He grabs the handrail but loses his footing.

Eight point four seconds after his first shot, Oswald fires for a third time. Jackie is leaning towards her husband's face.

> *And just as I turned and looked at him, I could see a piece of his skull and I remember it was flesh coloured. I remember thinking he just looked as if he had a slight headache. And I just remember seeing that. No blood or anything. And then he sort of put his hand to his forehead and fell in my lap. And then I just remember falling on him and saying, "Oh, no, no, no, Oh, my God, they have shot my husband.' I remember I was shouting. And just being down in the car with his head in my lap. And it just seemed an eternity.*
>
> *Jackie Kennedy testimony to the Warren Commission*
> *5th June 1964*

Associated Press photographer Ike Altgens is 15 feet away, his lens pointing at the car. Fragments of Kennedy's head are falling at his feet.

Six-year-old Jeff Franzen, standing with his parents, thinks confetti is coming out of the president's limo.

Clint Hill is making a final attempt to jump onto the back of the car and he gets a grip, just as Bill Greer hits the accelerator. Mrs Kennedy is crawling towards him, he thinks to catch something that's falling from the back of the car. He grabs her arm and pushes her back into the seat.

A few feet away, Charles Brehm throws himself over his young son – he knows gunfire having been shot in the chest on D-Day. As the car heads under the railway underpass Abraham Zapruder stops filming.

'They killed him! They killed him!' he yells. Kenny O'Donnell crosses himself as Dave Powers next to him mutters, 'Jesus, Mary and Joseph.'

On Elm Street Howard Brennan is watching the man at the sixth-floor window drawing his gun back and then pausing as if to check that he's hit his mark. Then he disappears. Brennan wants to scream but can't utter a sound.

> *I used to think if I only had been looking to the right I would have seen the first shot hit him, then I could have pulled him down, and then the second shot would not have hit him...*
>
> **Jackie Kennedy testimony to the Warren Commission**
> **5th June 1964**

Oswald is now running towards the staircase at the rear of the depository. He drops his rifle, scope up, between some large packing cases, puts another box on top to conceal it, and heads down the stairs.

Clint Hill is hanging onto the back of the speeding car, and he's watching a pitiful sight. Jackie Kennedy is cradling her husband's head in her lap saying, 'Jack, Jack, Jack. Can you hear me? I love you, Jack.' Through a windshield splattered with blood, the agents in the car behind are looking at Hill beating his hands on the trunk of the car in despair. He feels he should have taken the bullet.

In a radio car a short distance ahead of the president's limousine, Gary Delaune of KLIF Radio is shouting to his producer down the phone.

'Put me on, Phil! Put me on! Phil, am I on? We're here at the Trade Mart... The presidential car's coming up now. We can see Mrs Kennedy's pink suit, there's a Secret Service man spreadeagled over the top of the car, we can't see who's been hit, but apparently something is wrong here, something is terribly wrong...'

The large woman in the pink dress, so happy moments before, is vomiting against a street lamp.

Hugh Aynesworth of the *Dallas Morning News* has his hand in his pocket and is discovering that the only paper he has to take notes on are a couple of utility bills, and a letter from the Empire State Bank thanking him for opening an account. And he has no pen. Aynesworth spots a small boy with a giant pencil with a Stars and Stripes flag on the end, and gives him a couple of quarters for it. For the rest of the day this unlikely combination helps Aynesworth report on the biggest story of his career.

Some people are pointing to the railway yards nearby, and motorcycle policeman Clyde Haygood is running, gun in hand, up a grassy knoll towards the tracks. NBC's Robert MacNeil has jumped off the press bus and is running up the knoll too, thinking someone must have fired a gun as some sort of anti-Kennedy gesture.

Driving at 80 miles an hour, Bill Greer brings the limousine parallel with Chief Curry's lead car and yells, 'Take me to the hospital! Quick!' Curry heads for Parkland Hospital four miles away.

12.31pm

Robert MacNeil is beginning to realise that the policemen hunting in the railway tracks behind the knoll are looking in the wrong place. He heads for the nearest telephone.

Howard Brennan, clutching his hard hat, is running towards the depository. He spots a policeman and tells him that he saw a man in a window shoot the president. Reporter Hugh Aynesworth overhears the conversation.

'I saw him up there in that window. No doubt he was the one. He wasn't even in much of a hurry. I saw him real good.'

He starts giving a description, then notices Aynesworth, and asks the policeman to keep reporters away.

Oswald has got down as far as the second floor when he hears someone coming up the other way, and he darts into the lunchroom.

Face down on the floor of the car, Lyndon Johnson can see only Lady Bird's shoes. Agent Rufus Youngblood is still lying on top of him, his shortwave radio inches from Johnson's ear.

'He's hit! Hurry, he's hit! Let's get out of here!' a voice on the radio shouts.

Johnson can't make out the rest, but hears the word 'hospital'.

Policeman Marrion Baker had ridden his police motorbike straight to the front steps of the depository, and sprinted into the building past the manager Ron Truly. Now on the second floor, Baker sees Oswald walking away from him and draws his gun, shouting, 'Come here!' Truly has caught up with Baker, who asks him if he knows Oswald. Truly says he does, so Baker, convinced the gunman must be someone who doesn't belong in the building, turns and runs up the stairs.

Truly had taken Oswald on after Ruth Paine had called him and said that a 'fine young man' with a wife and young family urgently needed work. Truly likes Oswald, who's polite, well mannered, and always calls him 'sir'.

In Dealey Plaza, car salesman James Tague is talking to Deputy Sheriff Buddy Walters about what happened.

'You've got blood on your face. Where were you standing?' Walters says.

They walk towards the spot and are about to cross the street, when, through three lanes of traffic, Walters notices the kerb opposite has had a chip taken out of it. Standing over it, Tague and Walters look up and see that it lines up with the Book Depository.

12.32pm

Oswald is walking through the depository's second-floor office with a full bottle of Coke. Mrs Robert Reid, the clerical supervisor, tells him that the president has been shot 'but maybe they didn't hit him'. Oswald mumbles something and heads for the front entrance. She thinks it's strange for him to be in the second-floor office.

Robert MacNeil runs into the depository. He sees Oswald leaving and asks him where the nearest telephones are. Oswald points into the building where a man is on the phone and says, 'Better ask him', and walks off, heading for a bus that will take him to his rooming house in Marsalis. MacNeil misses a major scoop.

12.33pm

On switchboard position Number 2 at Parkland Hospital, Anne Ferguson is answering a call. A dispatcher shouts, '601 coming in on Code 3, stand by!'

601 is the call number of the president's motorcycle escort, Code 3 means extreme emergency.

Nellie Connally thinks her husband is dying and is whispering in his ear, 'It's going to be all right, be still.'

Behind her Jackie is saying, 'He's dead – they've killed him. Oh Jack, I love you.'

Her pink pillbox hat falls forward and she throws it on the floor of the car, the hatpin tearing out hair.

12.34pm

The United Press International (UPI) news printer spits out the first news of the assassination attempt, thanks to the quick reaction of their reporter Merriman Smith, who was in the motorcade press car and had grabbed the portable radiotele-phone first.

Over the noise of police sirens and the wind, agent Rufus Youngblood is shouting at the vice president lying beneath him.

'I want you and Mrs Johnson to stick with me and the other agents as close as you can. We are going into the hospital and we aren't gonna stop for anything or anybody. Do you understand?'

'Okay, partner, I understand,' Johnson replies.

12.35pm

Admiral Burkley, the President's doctor, is clambering into a police car at the Trade Mart. He's the only person who knows about the medications Kennedy takes. Chuck Roberts of *Newsweek* asks if he can go with him. The Admiral slams the door in his face. As they speed to the hospital, Burkley's hands are shaking.

'I want the world to see what Dallas has done to my husband.'

12.36pm

The president's limousine screeches to a halt by the Emergency Room entrance at the rear of Parkland. Clint Hill slides off the trunk. Governor Connally is still being cradled by Nellie, President Kennedy by Jackie. The hospital isn't ready – there's no one outside ready to help. Secret Service agents surround the car, some with submachine guns.

Merriman Smith arrives at Parkland just after the president's car. Smith sees Clint Hill.

'How is he?'

'He's dead, Smitty...'

Smith heads inside the hospital to find a phone so he can call UPI.

Dave Powers, JFK's aide and friend for nearly 20 years, is rushing over to the car, ignoring an agent calling him to stop. When he sees the horror of the back seat, he falls on the president and bursts into tears. The seat is covered in blood and there's a fragment of skull next to JFK. There are bits of tissue and brain matter everywhere. Jackie is holding her husband's head and weeping. Kenny O'Donnell can't bear to look.

Clint Hill pleads with her to allow them to get the president to a doctor.

'I'm not going to let him go, Mr Hill. You know he's dead. Let me alone,' she says quietly.

Hill realises why the first lady won't move – she wants to hide her husband's bloody body from the gathering crowd. Hill takes off his suit jacket and places it over the president's head and chest.

'It's okay now, Mrs Kennedy. Let us get him to the hospital.'

Jackie looks at Hill and nods. He sees her face is spattered with blood.

Governor Connally is being moved first, and begins to regain consciousness as he's put on a stretcher.

On ABC Radio, Doris Day is singing 'Hooray for Hollywood'. Suddenly newsreader Don Gardiner cuts in with Merriman Smith's UPI scoop.

'We interrupt this programme to bring you a special bulletin from ABC Radio. Here is a special bulletin from Dallas, Texas. Three shots were fired at President Kennedy's motorcade today in downtown Dallas, Texas. Stay tuned to your ABC station for further details. Now we return you to your regular programme...'

> *You always think of her... as being insulated, protected; she was quite alone. I don't think I ever saw anyone so much alone in my life. I went up to her, put my arms around her, and said to her something like, 'God help us all.'*
>
> **Lady Bird Johnson statement for the Warren Commission**
> **July 1964**

12.37pm

The Dallas Police are sealing all entrances to the Book Depository.

The Secret Service are running into the Emergency Room – people, seeing the submachine guns, hit the floor. Then the president is wheeled in, with Jackie holding his hand. Her pink hat and red roses are on his chest. A nurse suggests that she wipe the blood off her clothing.

'Absolutely not. I want the world to see what Dallas has done to my husband.'

Dave Powers scribbles in his notebook: 'I carried my President on stretcher. Ran to Emergency Room #1 (10x15ft.). Jackie ran beside stretcher holding on.'

Ralph Yarborough is talking to some reporters.
'Gentlemen there has been a deed of horror.'
Then he adds quietly, 'Excalibur has sunk beneath the waves...'

In grey tiled Trauma Room One, 34-year-old surgeon Dr Malcolm Perry rushes in from the canteen, still chewing his lunch. Throwing his jacket on the bloody floor, his first thought is that the president looks taller than he thought he would be; his second is 'here is the most important man in the world'.

Diana Hamilton-Bowron, a 22-year-old nurse, newly arrived from England, is cutting away JFK's clothes and back brace, and removing his bloody gold wristwatch. She puts the watch in her pocket for safekeeping. The president's body is covered with petals. His face is blue-white and his breathing spasmodic. His eyes are open and staring. Anaesthetist Dr Marion Jenkins thinks that the president has 'a death look'.

A plastic endotracheal tube connected to an automatic respirator has been inserted into Kennedy's mouth and down into his windpipe. It's clear to Dr Perry that it isn't working – air is leaking from a small wound in his throat. Perry then makes a large incision in the wound and inserts a tracheotomy tube.

Dr Conrad Peters looks at the bandages that JFK had wrapped round his middle that morning at the Hotel Texas, and thinks how odd it is for the president of the United States to be wearing a $3 dressing.

By now there are six doctors trying to keep the president alive, watched by Secret Service agents and Kennedy aides.

Outside the Trauma Room, Jackie Kennedy is sitting on a chair. Opposite her is Nellie Connally, also sitting and waiting. Nurse Doris Nelson offers to get Jackie a towel and to help her remove her blood-saturated gloves.

'No, thank you, I'm alright,' she replies.

Standing guard outside the Trauma Room is Sergeant Bob Dugger. He's looking so impassive and stern that Jackie wonders if he might dislike her husband. In fact Dugger is a Kennedy Democrat, who served in the Navy on torpedo boats, and is thinking, 'Why wasn't I killed instead of the president?' He doesn't know what to say to Mrs Kennedy.

In Trauma Room Two, the doctors are examining John Connally's wounds. He appears to have bullet wounds in his right-rear shoulder, under his right nipple, right wrist and left thigh, but there is so much blood it's hard to tell.

'How many times was he shot?' Dr Tom Shires asks.

'Once!' Connally says, and the medics all jump, as they thought he was unconscious. The governor finally gets some sedation.

Shires examines Connally's bloody head, looking for another wound, but then realises the blood and matter belong to President Kennedy.

> *[Oswald] said, 'And I want my room cleaned and clean sheets put on the bed.' And I said, 'Well, I will after you move because you are going to move.' He said, 'Why?' I says, 'Because I am not going to rent to you any more...' I didn't like his attitude. He was just kind of like this, you know, just big shot, you know, and I didn't have anything to say to him, I didn't like him... just didn't want him around me.*
>
> **Mary Bledsoe testimony to the Warren Commission**
> **2nd April 1964**

12.39pm

Mary Bledsoe is sitting on a bus heading towards the Dallas suburb of Marsalis, pleased at having seen the president ten minutes before. It's stuck in traffic and suddenly there's a loud banging on the door; the driver lets on a man who Mary recognises instantly as Lee Harvey Oswald, a tenant who'd rented a room from her the month before. He looks dirty, with a hole in the elbow of his shirt and with a face 'like a maniac'. She deliberately doesn't catch his eye as he walks down the aisle.

Mary never liked Oswald and asked him to leave the room he'd rented, after only a week. His comings and goings disturbed her afternoon naps and he spoke on the phone in a foreign language. When he left, she wished him 'good luck' but muttered 'good riddance'.

The bus is now stuck in traffic and Oswald gets off.

Kenny O'Donnell is standing next to Jackie outside the Trauma Room. They hear one of the medical team inside say 'resuscitation'. Suddenly she's hopeful.

'Do you think...?' she starts to say to O'Donnell. He says nothing.

12.40pm/6.40pm GMT

In the CBS studios in New York, the popular soap opera *As The World Turns* is being transmitted live across America. Actress Helen Wagner who is playing Nancy Hughes says, 'And I gave it a great deal of thought, Granp...' Suddenly there is a caption on the screen saying, 'CBS News Bulletin', followed by the voice of news anchor Walter Cronkite.

'Here is a bulletin from CBS News. In Dallas, Texas, three shots were fired at President Kennedy's motorcade in downtown Dallas.'

When he finishes, the network cuts to a coffee advertisement.

Marina Oswald and Ruth Paine are watching the bulletin. Marina's English isn't good enough to understand everything that Cronkite's saying, and she's full of questions.

'Was it serious? Is Jackie safe?'

Ruth is translating and weeping as she does so.

At Granada Television in Manchester, it's a quiet evening with only news editor Terry Dobson and his secretary Joan Riley in the newsroom. Dobson's phone is ringing. Joan can see it's a direct call, not one via the switchboard. Terry answers it, hears the news of the shooting in Dallas, and then picks up the internal phone to Barry Heads, the executive producer of *Scene at 6.30*, the regional news show currently going out live to the North-West. Heads tells him to verify the assassination story with the Press Association.

12.42pm

Merriman Smith is on the line to UPI, ignoring a nurse repeatedly saying, 'You can't use this phone!' NBC's Robert MacNeil has found a phone of his own and is persuading a hospital intern to hold onto it, while he gets updates from the stunned Kennedy aides.

12.43pm /1.43pm EST/6.43pm GMT

It's a warm November day in Virginia, and the president's brother, Attorney General Robert Kennedy, his wife Ethel and two colleagues are having lunch at home by the pool. Workmen are busy painting a new wing that's been added to the house. Suddenly one of the men runs towards the Kennedys holding a transistor radio in his hand, shouting something none of them can understand. The phone then rings and Ethel answers. The White House operator says, 'The director is calling.' Ethel tells her that her husband is busy at lunch, but the operator insists that it's urgent.

'It's J Edgar Hoover,' Ethel calls to her husband. Kennedy knows instantly there's a problem, as Hoover never rings him at home.

'I have news for you. The president's been shot,' the director of the FBI says flatly. Kennedy asks if it's serious.

'I think it's serious. I am endeavouring to get details. I'll call you back when I find out more.'

Kennedy staggers towards his wife.

'Jack's been shot! It may be fatal...'

At Granada Studios, Terry Dobson has verification about the shooting. Barrie Heads immediately dictates the news on talkback to the *Scene at 6.30* floor manager, who hands it to the presenter Mike Scott, who then reads it live to camera. This is the first news that a British audience has of the shooting. The other ITV networks are running a recorded pop show – *Ready Steady Go!,* but will later replace their scheduled programmes with news bulletins and recorded music. (The BBC will later receive complaints that after their announcement of the death of JFK, they ran *The Harry Worth Show* and *Dr Finlay's Casebook* as normal.)

12.44pm

In the Dallas Police Department, dispatcher Gerald Henslee has Howard Brennan's description in his hands. He broadcasts it over the police radio:

'Attention all squads, attention all squads, the suspect in the shooting at Elm and Houston is reported to be an unknown white male, approximately 30; slender build; height five feet, ten inches; weight 165 pounds, reported to be armed with what is thought to be a rifle...'

A receptionist is asking Nellie Connally, who is still sitting outside Trauma Room Two, to come to the office to fill out a hospital admission form for her husband. Nellie ignores her.

Lyndon and Lady Bird Johnson are in a cubicle at Parkland. He is leaning against the wall; she is sitting on a folding chair. They are looking at each other but neither of them is speaking. Johnson is wearing a white carnation given to him that morning at the Chamber of Commerce breakfast at Fort Worth.

Agents have pulled down the window blinds. One agent is outside the door, three more are inside with the Johnsons. Secret Service agent Rufus Youngblood is standing by the vice president, refusing to leave his side until he believes they are safe. He has tried to persuade Johnson to leave the hospital and fly to Washington on Air Force One, but Johnson wants to wait for news of the president.

12.45pm

Clint Hill and Roy Kellerman are talking to Jerry Behn, head of the Secret Service detail in the White House, when Robert Kennedy comes on the line. His voice sounds so similar to the president's that Clint Hill has to hold on to a wall for support.

'How bad is it?' he asks Hill.

From what he's witnessed in the car, Clint knows his brother is dead, but closes his eyes and says simply, 'It's as bad as it can get'.

Kennedy asks Hill how Jackie is coping, and then tells him to find a priest for his brother.

In downtown Dallas, William Whaley is halfway out of his 1961 Checker cab, about to get some cigarettes, when he sees a potential fare walking down the street waving at him. Lee Harvey Oswald asks, 'May I have a cab, sir?' and if he could be taken to 500 North Beckley. In the Russian fashion, Oswald sits next to the driver.

As they travel, Whaley comments on the police sirens,

wondering what's going on. Oswald looks at him but says nothing for the six-minute journey. Whaley thinks, 'Here's a guy who wants to be alone...'

On Dallas station WFAA-TV, a discussion on *The Julie Benell Show* about winter coats is replaced by panting programme director Jay Watson, who has just witnessed the shooting in Dealey Plaza and run four blocks to the studio.

'Good afternoon, ladies and gentlemen, you'll excuse the fact that I'm out of breath, but about ten or 15 minutes ago a tragic thing by all indications has happened in the city of Dallas...'

Marina Oswald is hanging out washing in the back yard. Ruth Paine, who has carried on watching the TV coverage, comes out to tell her that the shots were fired from the Book Depository. Ruth is excited at the thought that Lee might have seen something, but Marina is horrified by the news.

When Ruth goes inside, Marina heads to the garage where she knows Lee has hidden a rifle. She discovered it in March, and was shocked that her husband could buy such a thing when they were so short of money.

One Sunday afternoon a few days later, in their back yard, he'd asked her to take a picture of him. He disappeared into the house and returned dressed in black and holding the rifle in one hand and two newspapers in the other; in the waistband of his trousers was a revolver. Marina had laughed at him, and after he'd shown her how to operate the camera, she'd taken a picture (in fact she'd taken two by mistake). She asked Lee why he wanted his picture taken with guns 'of all stupid things'. He said he wanted to send it to the radical newspaper the *Militant*, to show them he was 'ready for anything'.

The following day he handed one of the photographs to Marina and told her to keep it for the baby. Marina saw that he'd written, 'For Junie from Papa.'

'Good God! Why would Junie want a picture with guns?' Marina asked.

'To remember Papa by sometime.'

Marina knows that Lee has the potential to kill. On 10th April he'd arrived home late, pale, and covered in sweat. He said he'd shot former US Army Major General Edwin Walker as he sat in his study. (Walker leads a radical militia group, who believe that communists are plotting to undermine American society.) In fact, Oswald had narrowly missed Walker, skimming his head and making a hole in the wall behind him. Marina said that no matter who he was, it wasn't right to try to kill him.

'Who is General Walker? Does he have a wife and family?'

'He's a fascist. If someone had killed Hitler in time, many lives would have been spared,' Oswald replied.

With a sigh of relief, Marina sees the green and brown wool blanket Lee wraps the rifle in, still bundled up on the floor, bound with string and looking as it did when she'd last seen the rifle three weeks before.

12.46pm/1.46pm EST

Ted Kennedy is on the dais at the Senate presiding over a debate on federal library services, when a press officer runs up to him.

'Your brother… your brother the president has been shot…'

Kennedy gathers up his papers and heads out of the building.

Liz Pozen, a friend of Jackie's, is driving her daughter Agatha and five-year-old Caroline Kennedy to their house for a sleepover. Caroline has brought with her a suitcase and her pink teddy bear. She's excited, as she's never stayed away from home before. Following the station wagon is Secret Service agent Tom Wells, a member of what is nicknamed the Kiddie Detail. Liz turns on the radio for some music, only to hear an announcer say, '...shot in the head and his wife Jackie...' She instantly turns it off, before Caroline can hear. Liz prays it's a hoax like Orson Welles' *War of the Worlds*. She looks in her rear view mirror to see if there's any sign Tom Wells has heard something.

Jackie Kennedy is walking into the Trauma Room with Admiral Burkley. The room goes quiet, the doctors suddenly more conscious of what they are doing.

Nurse Nelson had tried to stop Jackie coming through, feeling it better for her not to see the graphic medical procedures.

'I want to be there when he dies,' she'd insisted.

Jackie walks round her husband's body, hands clasped in front of her. She nudges Dr Ron Jones with her elbow and gives him some brain tissue; he passes it to a nurse.

12.50pm/1.50pm EST

Richard Nixon is in a cab in New York heading home. The driver has taken a wrong turning and ended up in Queens. Nixon flew out of Love Field that morning, two hours before JFK landed. The cab is waiting at a red light when suddenly a woman runs out of her house screaming and crying. Nixon winds down the window and asks her what's the matter. She recognises Nixon and turns pale, then tells him that Kennedy has been shot in Dallas. The light changes and the cab moves off. Nixon and the driver are silent for the rest of the journey.

FBI agent James Hosty is eating a cheese sandwich at the

counter of the Oriental Café in Dallas. The radio is on.

'Oh, my God, they've shot the president!' a waitress cries.

Hosty throws down a couple of dollars and heads for the door.

12.51pm

Cab driver William Whaley is dropping Oswald off a short distance from his lodgings. Oswald says nothing as he pays $1 for the 95-cent ride.

Twenty-four-year-old Englishman John Ravenscroft (later known as DJ John Peel) is reading in the toilets of the Republic National Life Insurance Company where he works in downtown Dallas. The PA system suddenly comes on, announcing to the staff that the president has been shot. Ravenscroft had met Kennedy three years before when he came to the city as a presidential candidate. They had chatted about why an Englishman would be working in Dallas, and Kennedy had then posed for a photo. Ravenscroft is shocked to hear his colleagues break into applause when they hear the news of the shooting.

12.52pm

Standing in the Emergency Room corridor, hospital administrator Steve Landregan overhears Earle Cabell, the city's mayor, saying to himself, 'It didn't happen! It didn't happen...!'

12.54pm

Book Depository manager Ron Truly is watching the police taking the names and addresses of his stockboys. He suddenly realises that one of them is missing, and yet he saw him barely

20 minutes ago...

12.55pm/1.55pm EST

Agent Tom Wells is driving Caroline back to the White House. The trip to Liz Pozen's house is off. He'd heard news of the assassination on the radio and had called the White House for instructions, but the phone lines were tied up. Wells fears that America might be in the middle of a coup and he wants to get Caroline to a secure location as quickly as possible.

Suddenly he's aware that a driver alongside him in a green sedan has recognised the president's daughter – the most photographed child in America – and so Wells speeds off. The man, who probably suspects Wells (in an unmarked car) of kidnapping Caroline in the aftermath of the shooting, gives chase. As they race through the Washington streets, the sedan is only a few feet away from Wells' rear bumper. Five minutes away from the White House, Wells finally loses the sedan.

Outside Parkland, groups of people are on their knees praying.

Bert Shipp of WFAA-TV asks Sheriff Decker, 'What's it look like, Sheriff?'

'Well, did you ever see a deer hit in the back of the head? There's nothing back there.'

'He can't live like that,' replies Shipp.

1.00pm/2.00pm EST

A cardiac monitor has been attached to the president and Dr Perry is performing a heart massage, kneeling on a stool.

'I think you'd better look at this,' Dr Jenkins tells Dr Kemp Clark, pointing to Kennedy's head wound. Clark, the hospital's chief neurosurgeon, looks at the wound – the first time anyone has done so. He can see instantly that their fight to save the president is over.

'It's too late, Mac,' he says to Perry, who keeps pumping the chest. 'No, Malcolm, we're through.'

Lee Harvey Oswald is leaving his boarding house with a light grey jacket to cover the snub-nosed .38 Smith & Wesson tucked into the waist of his trousers.

A sheet is pulled up over the body.

'I think we need to find Mrs Kennedy,' Dr Peters says. Someone signals that she's standing behind him. Dr Charles Baxter, the chief of the Emergency Room, says, 'Mrs Kennedy, your husband is dead. We will not pronounce him dead until he's had the last rites.'

The medical team removes the tubes and monitoring equipment, back away from the body, and then leaves the room.

Jackie kisses her husband's foot, stomach and lips. She starts to cry.

Dr Baxter would say later that 'there were probably more tears shed in that room than in the surrounding hundred miles'.

Clint Hill is on the phone to Oneal's Funeral Home.

'We've got merchandise at all prices,' Vernon Oneal says.

'Bring the best one you have. Any questions?'

Oneal goes to select his most expensive casket, but knows that he's going to have to wait until his staff come back from their lunch break before he can get the $4,000 solid-bronze 'Britannia' model into the hearse.

Dave Powers scribbles in his notebook, 'One o'clock. My president is dead.'

Hospital administrator Steve Landregan gives Hill his own jacket to cover up the agent's bloody shirt. Dave Powers notices the blood on his suit but doesn't care – it's a cheap one. As he often says to his wife, when you travel with the president, no one notices what you wear.

WNEW-News Radio reporter Ike Pappas is coming out of the New York subway at West Fourth Street and a woman is running up to him screaming and crying, 'The president has been shot! The president has been shot!'

Pappas walks away saying to himself, 'When the tourists come out tonight, lady, you can tell them that story. I don't believe it.' But then he looks around and senses electricity in the air – New Yorkers are talking to each other; some are listening to transistor radios. 'What if it's true?' he thinks, as he runs for the nearest phone.

In Los Angeles, freeways have ground to a halt as the drivers, having heard the news on their car radios, pull over to take it in.

1.05pm

Father Oscar Huber of Holy Trinity Catholic Church has just arrived. He'd received a call from the hospital administrator and rushed straight over. Jackie watches as he uncovers the sheet that hides her husband's face.

'Si capax, ego te absolvo a peccatis tuis, in nomine Patris, et Filii, et Spiritus Sancti. Amen.' 'If it is possible, I absolve you from your sins in the name of the Father and of the Son and of the Holy Ghost. Amen.'

He then presses his thumb in holy oil and anoints Kennedy's forehead with the sign of the cross. An hour ago he'd been cheering the president from the sidewalk.

1.06pm/2.06pm EST

Ike Pappas didn't have to ask about the president when he got through to the WNEW newsroom; the noise in the background was enough to tell him the screaming woman wasn't lying.

'What's this about Kennedy..?' he asks.

'Get your ass up here,' the producer at the other end says.

1.07pm

Bob Huffaker of local radio station KRLD News is broadcasting live.

'Hundreds of people crowd outside the back door of the Emergency Room here at Parkland Hospital. Faces are ashen white. And people are wondering, "Is our president going to live?"'

1.10pm

'Thank you for taking care of the president. Please pray for him,' Jackie is saying to Father Huber.

As he's about to leave the hospital an agent says to the priest firmly, 'Father, you don't know anything about this.'

He nods in agreement.

John Ravenscroft is on Elm Street watching policemen search the grassy knoll. He'd left work as soon as he'd heard the news of the shooting and driven as close as he could to Dealey Plaza. At a roadblock a sobbing policeman had stopped him, but after Ravenscroft said he was from the *Liverpool Echo*, he'd allowed him through.

1.12pm

Deputy Sheriff Luke Mooney is on the sixth floor of the depository, squeezed between two tall stacks of boxes. On the floor he spots three spent cartridge casings. Then he notices a slight crease in one of the boxes – it looks like a perfect place to steady a rifle. Mooney leans out of the sixth-floor window and shouts to his colleagues.

Outside Parkland, a crowd of reporters is surrounding Father Huber.

'Is he dead?'

'He's dead all right,' Huber replies.

1.13pm

Police patrolman JD Tippit is driving along Tenth Street in Dallas in his '63 Ford cruiser. He's an experienced cop, who six years earlier had been stabbed in the stomach and knee by a man with an ice pick. The encounter gave him a limp and a more cautious approach to policing – which his wife Marie welcomed.

Tippit can see ahead of him a man walking briskly who matches the description of the assassin that's just come over the radio. He pulls the patrol car over to the side of the road and calls to the man. Oswald stops and leans on the car, and they speak through the vent in the window. Something in their exchange makes Tippit suspicious and he gets out. As he reaches the front of the car, Oswald pulls out his revolver and shoots him four times in the head and the stomach. Officer Tippit's cap rolls out into the street.

Just half a block away, waitress Helen Markham, waiting for a bus to take her to work in downtown Dallas, is watching, horrified. Oswald walks towards her, playing with his gun.

> **He didn't run. It just didn't scare him to death. He didn't run. When he saw me he looked at me, stared at me. I put my hands over my face like this, closed my eyes. I gradually opened my fingers like this, and I opened my eyes, and when I did he started off in kind of a little trot...**
>
> **Helen Markham testimony to the Warren Commission**
> **26th March 1964**

1.14pm

Sisters-in-law Virginia and Barbara Davis heard the gunshots and are standing at their front door watching Oswald smile at them as he runs across the lawn, emptying spent cartridges out of his gun.

Taxi driver William Scoggins had seen Tippit being shot, and is now hiding behind his car. He thinks he might be next. As Oswald passes he hears him mutter, 'Poor dumb cop, poor dumb cop...'

Mechanic Domingo Benavides is in Tippit's squad car using the radio to call for help. A small crowd has gathered around the policeman who's lying dead on the ground with his gun still in his hand.

'Hello, police operator?'

'Go ahead. Go ahead citizen using police radio.'

'We've had a shooting out here.'

'Where's it at?'

'On Tenth Street, between Marsalis and Beckley. It's a police officer. Somebody shot him.'

'Seventy-eight,' the dispatcher says, trying to call Tippit.

'It's a police car. Number Ten. You got that?'

'Seventy eight... Seventy eight?' the dispatcher repeats.

The Hollywood actress Joan Crawford is speaking to a secretary at the Parkland Hospital, requesting that a message be passed to Mrs Kennedy asking if she needs any assistance.

1.15pm

Used-car salesman Ted Callaway has grabbed Tippit's service revolver and persuaded a reluctant William Scoggins to 'get the son of a bitch responsible for this!' Scoggins is so nervous he's taking ages to turn the car around. Callaway is shouting, 'C'mon, fella, let's move! C'mon, let's go!'

On CBS, reporter Eddie Barker is telling viewers that President Kennedy is dead.

'The word we have is from a doctor on the staff of Portland Hospital who says that it is true. He was in tears when he told me just a moment ago...'

1.20pm

Technician Darrell Tomlinson can see a trolley blocking a narrow corridor in the Emergency Room and so he pushes it back towards the wall. (It's the trolley that was used to move Governor Connally to an operating theatre 30 minutes before.) As it hits the wall Tomlinson hears a clink and spots a bullet lying against the metal rim. He calls over OP Wright, an ex-cop now working as a personnel officer at the hospital. Wright is unable to find an FBI agent willing to look at the bullet, so he puts it in his pocket.

Secret Service agent Sam Kinney has got the bubbletop out

of the boot of the Lincoln and is fixing it on. He's struck by the bitter irony that instead of protecting passengers from the weather, its job now is to protect a crime scene. Kinney has to drive the car to the Air Force cargo plane at Love Field that will take it on to Washington.

Clint Hill walks outside, sees the midnight-blue car, and flinches.

Book Depository manager Ron Truly is on the phone to the warehouse where job application forms are kept. He's jotting down Lee Harvey Oswald's contact details, which are the phone number and address of Ruth Paine. He hands them to a policeman and together they take the elevator to the sixth floor where Captain Will Fritz, the chief of Homicide and Robbery, is coordinating the search for evidence.

Kenny O'Donnell is walking into the hospital cubicle where Lyndon Johnson is waiting. O'Donnell looks stricken.

'He's gone,' he says.

1.22pm

Waitress Helen Markham is describing Tippit's murder to half a dozen reporters. Someone has given her an empty Coca-Cola case to sit on.

'I was screaming for someone to help me. I kept saying, 'Somebody has killed a policeman! He has killed him! Killed him! Oh God, Help us!''

1.23pm

Press secretary Mac Kilduff needs to speak to Lyndon Johnson urgently.

'Mr President...'

Johnson looks up in surprise. It's the first time he's been addressed like that.

1.25pm

The FBI and Secret Service cleared the emergency area of press fifteen minutes ago, but missed Robert MacNeil standing behind the door of the waiting room. Lyndon Johnson is striding through, surrounded by Secret Service agents, and MacNeil steps in front of him.

'Is the president dead?'

Johnson, looking very pale, stops, stares and says nothing, then almost knocks MacNeil over as he heads for the exit.

1.26pm

The new president and his Secret Service detail are rushing from the back of Parkland, towards a police car waiting outside, which will take them to Air Force One.

The flag outside the hospital is at half-mast.

The English nurse Diana Hamilton-Bowron realises she has the president's gold wristwatch in her pocket. She runs out of Trauma One to find Jack Price, the hospital administrator. He gives it to a Secret Service agent.

1.27pm

Agent Roy Kellerman is in the nurse's station on the line to the White House. A man walks in and says to him, 'I am the Dallas County medical examiner, Earl Rose. There's been a homicide here; you won't be able to remove the body. We will have to take it down there to the mortuary and have an autopsy.'

'No, you are not.'

"Well, we have a law here whereby you have to comply with it…'

Admiral Burkley walks in and Kellerman explains the situation.

'Doctor, this man is from some health unit in town. He tells me we can't remove this body…"

Burkley loses it.

'We *are* removing the body! This is the president of the United States and there should be some consideration in an event like this!' An autopsy means that Mrs Kennedy would have to remain in Dallas for at least another 24 hours, and that is intolerable.

Kellerman remains cool and turns to Earl Rose.

'You are going to have to come up with someone a little stronger than you, to give me the law that this body can't be removed.'

Rose heads for a phone. He fully intends to find someone who will make these men realise that Texas law is on his side.

As they speed through the streets of Dallas in Chief Curry's car, agent Rufus Youngblood asks him to turn off his siren; he doesn't want to attract unnecessary attention. President Johnson is crouched down behind the driver, Youngblood by the window on the other side of the back seat, where the vice president would normally sit. If there is an assassin at large in Dallas, he will take the bullet.

1.30pm/2.30pm EST/7.30pm GMT

Radio reporter Travis Linn is in a car driving back from the Trade Mart where the president had been due to give a speech. As he passes Dealey Plaza he remembers the tape recorder he asked AJ L'Hoste to leave there, to capture the sound of the motorcade. He asks to be dropped off.

The Secret Service detail at the White House are drawing lots to decide who tells Maud Shaw, the Kennedy children's English nanny, that the president has died. Agent Bob Foster loses.

On stage at London's Old Vic, before the start of a National Theatre production of *Uncle Vanya*, Lawrence Olivier is asking the audience to join him in singing 'The Star Spangled Banner'. Three years earlier, Olivier had performed in Washington at JFK's inaugural gala.

1.33pm

Parkland's nurses' classroom has been converted into a make-shift pressroom. White House press officer Mac Kilduff is in front of the blackboard trying to summon up the courage to speak. He's pale and the reporters can see that he's trying not to cry, but his cheeks are already covered in tears.
'Excuse me, let me catch my breath...'
A full minute passes as he tries to think of how to say the words. Reporter Robert MacNeil can see that his hands are shaking and he's trying to steady them by pressing down hard on the desk in front of him.

Mrs Leonora Jenkins hasn't heard from her reporter son Ron for over a year. She's watching the press conference on TV and can see Ron's hand holding out a microphone to catch Kilduff's words. She knows it's Ron as soon as she sees the watch she and her husband gave him for his high school graduation. Mrs Jenkins is relieved to know that he's all right.

Oswald's rifle was found 15 minutes ago, hidden between some boxes. An initial dusting by Lieutenant Carl Day of the Crime Search Unit failed to find any fingerprints, so he plans to take it back to his lab for more careful analysis. Day holds the gun while Captain Fritz pulls the bolt back. A live round falls to the floor.

With them on the sixth floor of the depository is *Dallas Morning News* journalist Kent Biffle, who's excited to be at the centre of this global story, but also wary of the armed police officers around him, who, having heard of Tippit's death, are nervous and jumpy. As Biffle steps out of an office, two policemen at either end of the corridor draw their guns.

Mac Kilduff has found the words.
'President John F Kennedy... President John F Kennedy died at approximately one o'clock Central Standard Time today here in Dallas. He died of gunshot wounds in the brain...'
Hospital staff leap out of the way as some of the reporters run from the room for the nearest phones.

1.34pm

Ruth and Marina are sitting on the sofa weeping at the news that the president is dead.
'What a terrible thing for Mrs Kennedy, and for the children to be left without a father,' Marina says.

Bob Huffaker of KRLD News is almost alone in the Parkland

pressroom. He and Mac Kilduff stare at each other in silence.

'This is one briefing I never thought I'd give,' Kilduff says.

Kilduff has been fired by Kenny O'Donnell. A few days before they left Washington, he told Kilduff that he should take up a position elsewhere as they had to lose a member of the press team. When Kilduff mentioned to JFK that he was having to leave, the president said, 'Forget it. I'll take care of it when we get back from Texas.'

Now he's lost his champion.

1.38pm

Vernon Oneal has arrived with the casket in one of his white hearses (he believes that death should never be depressing). Clint Hill is signing for it.

Dallas Morning News nightclub reporter Tony Zoppi had arrived late at Parkland and been unable to get past the police cordon as he'd forgotten his press pass. He's watching Oneal's men and Secret Service agents struggle with the heavy casket. The driver of the hearse suddenly calls to him.

'Grab a corner, will you?'

So Zoppi helps carry the casket onto a trolley. As they get close to the hospital doors, he starts to move away, but the agents tell him to keep pushing. Almost without thinking, Zoppi reaches under the casket and pushes his hand hard against it to make some fingerprints. He reckons the president will soon be inside the casket and he wants him to know that Tony Zoppi helped carry it in, if nothing else. But he'll never fully explain why he did it.

Following a yellow line on the floor, Zoppi pushes the casket to the Trauma Room door, where a Secret Service agent says,

'We'll take it from here, gentlemen.'

'Oh, no, we got...' says Zoppi.

'We'll take it from here.'

Zoppi doesn't push his luck.

1.39pm

Jackie is walking behind funeral director Vernon Oneal as he brings the casket into Trauma Room One. Sergeant Dugger, at last feeling that he can do something useful for the former first lady, helps her take off a glove. Jackie then removes her wedding ring and puts it on her husband's ring finger on his left hand.

Later, in the corridor, she asks Kenny O'Donnell, 'The ring. Did I do the right thing?'

'You leave it right where it is,' he reassures her.

1.42pm

A transistor radio is on in Hardy's Shoe Store, Oak Cliff, Dallas. For the past hour the manager Johnny Brewer has been listening to news reports about the assassination. A few minutes ago they announced that a policeman had been shot just up the road.

A man is walking into the entrance of the store as a police car passes, siren blaring. Brewer thinks it's strange that the man doesn't turn to see what's going on. He can see that he looks scared and out of breath. The man waits for a moment, looks at Brewer, then over his shoulder and heads off down the street. Suspicious, Brewer quickly follows him and sees the man dart into the Texas Theater, a cinema showing a double-bill of *Cry of Battle* and *War Is Hell*.

Tony Zoppi has one of the few phones that haven't been tied up by the FBI or Secret Service, and he's calling the *Dallas Morning News* office. He'd found a girl on a switchboard who'd let him use a phone in a nearby office, as she read his column every day. Johnny King, the city editor, answers.

'Johnny, this is Tony Zoppi. The president's dead.'

'How the hell do you know?'

'I just carried in his casket.'

'You better be right.'

'I'm right,' Zoppi says.

> *I stepped out of the box office and... as I turned around Johnny Brewer was standing there and he asked me if the fellow that ducked in bought a ticket, and I said, 'No, by golly, he didn't,'... and I said, 'Go in and see if you can see him, it isn't too much people in there...'*
>
> *Julia Postal testimony to the Warren Commission*
> *2nd April 1964*

1.45pm/2.45pm EST

Johnny Brewer and 'Butch' Burroughs, an usher at the Texas Theater, are checking the lock bars on the exit doors. They are all down, so they know the man Brewer followed is still in the building. They look into the auditorium but it's too dark to see who's in there. They hear a seat pop up.

In the box office, cashier Julia Postal calls the police, then phones the projectionist to check if he can see anything.

On US television, all adverts have been suspended until the president's funeral, and for the first time ever, the three networks have cancelled their regular programmes and are broadcasting only live news. On CBS, Walter Cronkite is reading some wire copy just handed to him.

'From Dallas, the flash apparently official, President Kennedy died at one o'clock Central Standard Time – some 38 minutes ago...' Cronkite pauses, swallows and puts on his glasses. A young journalist in shot behind him looks up from the Teletype machine that brought the news, to see why the famous newsman has stopped talking.

1.46pm

Travis Linn can see the tape recorder on top of one of the tall ornamental pedestals in Dealey Plaza. He grabs it and heads back to the WFAA studios to hear what it has recorded, if anything.

In the Book Depository, reporter Kent Biffle is listening to policemen discussing the death of Officer Tippit. At first they're despondent at the news, but then cheer up when they discover it's not the Tippit they thought it was. They don't know JD Tippit, who had tended to keep himself to himself.

'There the son of a bitch sits.'

1.47pm

Policemen are running into the Texas Theater, many of them brandishing guns. Some are staying outside to control a crowd that's growing by the minute. Shoe store manager Johnny Brewer is peering round a curtain by an exit, when the house lights come half up. He can see the man he followed get up from his seat and move to a row further back. Behind Brewer the exit door rattles, and he opens it only to be grabbed by a policeman who points a gun at his stomach.

1.50pm

Johnson has reached Love Field. He and agent Youngblood are running up the steps of Air Force One. Youngblood shouts for the blinds to be pulled down – he's worried about snipers. The plane is hot and stuffy as Colonel Swindal, preparing for a swift departure, has disconnected it from the air conditioning truck that keeps the plane cool on the ground.

Clint Hill is on the phone to Bob Foster, the lead agent on the Kiddie Detail. As they talk, Hill is thinking of the president's last words when he said goodbye to John Jr at Andrews Air Force Base: 'Take care of John for me, won't you, Mr Foster?'

John Jr had been crying because he'd wanted to fly with his parents and so Foster had distracted him with stories of Jasper the Jet, until he could see Air Force One had taken off. Foster had thought the president's request to him strange; John Jr always cried when his father left, and JFK had never made that remark before.

Johnny Brewer is on the stage of the Texas Theater pointing out to four policemen the man he'd seen in his store. They leave the stage, pretending instead to be interested in two men across the aisle from the suspect. Officer Nick McDonald asks them to stand and then searches them for weapons. He glances over his shoulder and can see the man sitting, watching him. McDonald suddenly turns and orders him to get to his feet.

'Well, it's all over now!' Oswald says. He lifts his hands in surrender and then punches McDonald between the eyes with his left fist. With his right hand Oswald pulls out his gun and McDonald grabs it, the skin between his thumb and forefinger caught between the hammer and the primer as Oswald then pulls the trigger.

Several other cops join in the struggle for the gun, including some who, only 20 minutes before, had been searching the Book Depository. Oswald is hit from behind with the butt of a shotgun and handcuffed.

'Kill the president, will you?' someone yells.

'Don't hit me any more. I am not resisting arrest! I know my rights, I want a lawyer!' Oswald shouts.

Reporters from the Dallas papers arrive in time to witness the arrest. The film *War Is Hell* is still flickering on the screen.

1.52pm

Parkland personnel officer OP Wright is giving the bullet found on the trolley to Secret Service agent Dick Johnsen. Johnsen looks at it and sees instantly it's been fired from a gun. He has to get Mrs Kennedy and the casket to Love Field, so he wraps the bullet in a handkerchief and puts it in his pocket.

On Air Force One, Lyndon Johnson is discussing with his aides whether he should be sworn in as president before they take off. Fearing a conspiracy and that Russia might take advantage of the situation, he decides he must take the oath now in Dallas.

1.54pm

There's a crowd of several hundred people now outside the Texas Theater. There are rumours that the president's killer has been captured. When he's led outside, Oswald shrinks back as they shout obscenities at him and scream, 'Let us have him. We'll kill him!'

'I protest this police brutality!' Oswald shouts back.

An old woman swats him with her umbrella.

Johnny Brewer is sprinting back to his shop – he realises he's left it open. A lot has happened in the 12 minutes since he left it.

1.56pm/2.56pm EST

The phone rings at Robert Kennedy's house. It's Lyndon Johnson calling from the bedroom on Air Force One, where he's lying on the bed. After expressing his condolences, Johnson asks Kennedy if he has any objections to him being sworn in right away, and who should do it. Stunned, Kennedy says that he'll get back to him with an answer.

1.58pm

At Parkland, Jackie Kennedy is smoking a cigarette as she waits for her husband's body. She asks Sergeant Dugger what's causing the delay. He pretends not to know, but has a hunch that Earl Rose, the medical examiner is trying to stop the president's body leaving the building for its journey to Air Force One.

In the Texas Theater box office, a policeman is using the phone while cashier Julia Postal listens in.

'I think we have got our man on both accounts.'

'What two accounts?' she asks when he hangs up. When the officer mentions the president and Officer Tippit, she's shocked as she knew Jefferson Tippit from when he used to work as a part-time security guard at the theatre.

2.00pm/3.00pm EST

Sergeant Dugger is right. About 40 men are crowded around the Emergency Room doors and a heated argument is going on between agent Kellerman and Earl Rose, who insists, correctly, that Texas law requires an autopsy. Rose, looking pale and agitated, has with him Theron Ward, a young justice of the peace for Dallas County whom he summoned to the hospital to back him up.

'Judge, do you know who I am? There must be something in your thinking here that we don't have to go through this agony, so the family doesn't have to go through this. We will take care of the matter when we get back to Washington,' Kellerman tells Ward.

'I know who you are. I can't help you out,' Ward says.

'Can't you make an exception for President Kennedy?' Kenny O'Donnell pleads.

'It's just another homicide case as far as I'm concerned,' Ward replies.

Robert Kennedy is on the phone to the new president. Johnson says he wants to know from him, as the attorney general, the precise wording for the oath of office. (What else was discussed during this call would be disputed by the two men. Johnson claimed Kennedy said the oath should be administered immediately, and that it could be administered by any judicial officer. Kennedy would always deny it.)

2.02pm

Oswald is sitting between two police officers in the back of a squad car.

'I know my rights. What is this all about?' Oswald asks. They tell him about the shooting of JD Tippit.

'Police officer been killed? I hear they burn for murder.'

'You may find out,' says Officer CT Walker.

Kenny O'Donnell and Roy Kellerman have had enough of arguing with Texans.

'We don't give a damn what these laws say. We're not staying here three hours or three minutes!' O'Donnell says. He looks at Sergeant Dugger, whose fists are doubled, ready to thump Earl Rose.

'Get out of the way, we're leaving!' O'Donnell shouts.

Secret Service agents push the casket and trolley past a furious Rose, shoving a policeman to one side. A crucifix placed on top almost falls off. Jackie follows, with a hand, still in a blood-stained glove, resting on the casket. Jack Price, the administrator for the hospital, instinctively reaches out and touches the casket as it passes, as a sort of final salute.

Clint Hill tells Jackie that they can ride in the car behind the hearse.

'No, Mr Hill, I'm riding with the president.'

Sergeant Dugger, still enraged and embarrassed by Earl Rose's behaviour, opens the door of the hearse for Jackie.

'Thank you,' she says.

He finally finds his voice.

'Bob Dugger, ma'am.'

2.05pm

Robert Oswald, 29, is at work in the marketing department of the Acme Brick Company in Denton, Texas. He's hurrying to his desk having dropped off some invoices when he hears someone say 'Oswald'. He stops, thinking someone is calling him, but then realises it's come from a transistor radio on the receptionist's desk. The receptionist is crying. Then the radio bulletin mentions the name in full.

'Lee Harvey Oswald has been arrested...'

'That's my kid brother!' Robert exclaims. A salesman leaning on a wall nearby says, 'Bob, let's not hope this is true.'

Detective Paul Bentley pulls a brown leather wallet from the suspect's left hip pocket.

'Lee Oswald,' he says, reading a Dallas Public Library card.

He says nothing. Bentley sees another name in the wallet.

'Alex J Hidell.'

Again, nothing.

'I guess we are going to have to wait until we get to the station to find out who he actually is,' says Bentley.

Reporter Kent Biffle, still in the Book Depository, hears an officer mention Lee Harvey Oswald as a suspect. He recognises the name. Four years earlier, Biffle had written stories about this 19-year-old ex-Marine who'd defected to Russia. He'd invited Oswald's mother Marguerite into the newsroom to make a phone call to her son in Moscow, but Oswald had refused to speak to her.

Squeezed in with the casket in the back of the hearse for the journey to Love Field, are Clint Hill, Admiral Burkley and Jackie Kennedy.

2.06pm

In the news studio of WFAA-TV, presenter Jay Watson is half listening to the director in his earpiece and half listening to an eye-witness to the shooting. He suddenly turns and gives the man his full attention when he describes the impact of the final bullet.

'I saw his head practically open up, all blood and everything and I kept on shooting. That's about all of it. I'm just sick of it, kid,' says Abraham Zapruder, as he fights back tears.

'You have film in your camera – we'll try and process it as soon as possible...' says Watson.

Robert Oswald is on the phone to his mother Marguerite, telling her to meet him at the Adolphus Hotel in Dallas that evening. It's the first time they've spoken in months; he hasn't seen Lee for almost a year.

On the sixth floor of the Book Depository, Lieutenant Carl Day is dusting for fingerprints. He's found none on the three empty rifle shells, none on the cracked paint of the windowsill and none on the gun. He's now working on one of the packing cases in the sniper's nest. Day has a hunch that the assassin used the box as a support while he waited for the motorcade. He's proved correct when a clear left palm print emerges. It suggests that the gunman was nervous, as the print was made by sweat.

2.08pm

Robert Oswald calls his wife Vada, suggesting that she goes with their two children to her parents' isolated farm in Boyd, outside Dallas. Robert doesn't say so to Vada, but he's worried about reprisals against his family.

2.10pm

The hearse is travelling at speed. Inside Admiral Burkley is fumbling for something. He produces two roses from the bouquet given to Jackie at Love Field.

'These were under... in his shirt' he says.

Jackie places them in the pocket of her pink suit.

A phone is ringing at the newsdesk of the Fort Worth *Star-Telegram*. Crime reporter Bob Schieffer answers, and a woman at the other end asks if there's anyone who could give her a lift to Dallas. Schieffer points out that they're a newspaper not a taxi service and that the president has been shot.

'Yes, I heard it on the radio. I think the person they've arrested is my son.'

Schieffer's jaw drops. He has a scoop and Marguerite Oswald has her lift into town.

2.12pm

From the top of one of Love Field's air cargo buildings, news cameraman Jimmy G Darnell is filming the president's casket being loaded on board Air Force One. He then climbs down the ladder on the outside of the building, and comes face to face with a Dallas policeman.

'Let me have that. That's sacrilegious.'

Darnell hands the film over and never sees it again.

Nellie Connally is receiving some good news. Surgeon Dr Robert Shaw (who had been airlifted by NASA from Houston to operate on her husband) says that the bullet missed his major arteries. He has a hole in his chest the size of a baseball, but will survive. Shaw praises Nellie for holding her husband's right arm across the wound as they sped to Parkland, as it shut off air to his chest. Nellie explains she was simply hugging her husband out of pure instinct.

2.14pm

President Kennedy had loved flying on Air Force One. He'd helped with its design, and when he saw the finished $8.6 million jet for the first time he'd joked, 'It's magnificent! I'll take it!'

There's no space on Air Force One for a casket, so four seats and a partition have been removed. At the foot of the aircraft's steps, Jackie Kennedy is watching the Secret Service agents, together with Kenny O'Donnell and Dave Powers, struggle to get the heavy casket inside. O'Donnell keeps looking over his shoulder expecting the Dallas medical authorities to arrive, still insisting on an autopsy. The casket won't fit through the rear door, so they break off its handles.

2.15pm

Captain Will Fritz of the Homicide Bureau is back at the Police Department in City Hall, and handing two of his officers an address in Irving, where he wants them to pick up a suspect named Lee Oswald. One of the officers points to a man who's just been brought in.

'Captain, we can save you a trip – there the son of a bitch sits.'

James Hosty is sitting in the Dallas FBI office running through possible right-wing suspects. His supervisor Ken Howe grabs his elbow.

'They've just arrested a guy named Lee Oswald, and they're booking him for the killing of a policeman over at Oak Cliff!'

Hosty recognises the name. Oswald had defected to the Soviet Union in 1959 and returned three years later with a Russian wife. He has files on both of them, as they are possible espionage risks. Since March, Hosty has been looking into Oswald's support for Fidel Castro's Cuba, and had been to Ruth Paine's house twice in November; he'd spoken briefly to Marina and had a longer conversation with Ruth. Hosty heads over to City Hall to help with the police interrogation of Oswald.

Travis Linn is in the dubbing suite of WFAA, transferring the audio from the tape recorder left at Dealey Plaza onto a more robust reel-to-reel machine. It's a good recording – he can hear the crowd cheering the motorcade. Then he hears a rifle shot, then another, and then after a pause, as if the gunman was taking proper aim, a third. The phone rings – it's the news director who's had a tip-off; he wants Linn to go to Lee Harvey Oswald's lodgings in Oak Cliff. As he leaves the dubbing suite Linn shouts, 'Don't erase that tape!'

2.16pm

In the Parkland classroom, Dr Malcolm Perry is being bombarded with questions by the press. He's barely finishing one answer before another question is yelled at him.

'[The president] was critically ill and moribund at the time these measures were begun.'

'Completely ill and what?'

'Moribund.'

'What does that mean?'

'Near death.'

'What was the word you used?'

'Moribund. Dr Clark arrived thereafter, immediately.'

'Could you tell us what resuscitative measures were attempted?'

'Assisted respiration.'

'What is that?'

'With what?'

'Assisted respiration with oxygen and an anaesthesia machine, passage of an endotracheal tube...'

'Does that mean you stick it in...?'

Perry's main concern had been to save the president's life and he hadn't done a full examination; he hadn't even turned the body over, so hadn't had the opportunity to fully examine the bullet wounds. Someone asks Perry to show where the neck wound was, and Perry points just below his Adam's apple. Pressed, he says that it 'appeared to be an entrance wound'. The reporters start scribbling that there's evidence Kennedy was hit from the front by at least one bullet.

2.18pm

Air Force One is dark and stuffy. Jackie is walking towards the president's bedroom; it's the last place that she and Jack had been alone together. As she walks in, Johnson, who had been dictating to his secretary Marie Fehmer, leaps off the bed and hurriedly leaves the cabin.

Roy Kellerman feels uneasy. He usually knows everyone on board Air Force One, but the plane is full of unfamiliar people, many from Air Force Two, the vice president's plane. From the way he is acting it's clear to Kellerman that Rufus Youngblood, Johnson's agent, feels that he's now in charge.

General Godfrey McHugh, JFK's air force aide, is feeling equally unsettled. He tells Mac Kilduff that they should take off immediately. Kilduff says that they're not flying to Washington 'until the president has been sworn'. McHugh flushes and says angrily, 'I have only one president, and he's lying back in that cabin.'

Kenny O'Donnell overhears, and is deeply proud of the General. He has little respect for Johnson.

JFK and O'Donnell used to have a set routine to deal with Johnson's many complaints. The president would listen to the vice president's grievance and then call in O'Donnell and tell him off in front of Johnson.

'Damn it, Kenny, you've gone and done it again!'

O'Donnell would meekly take the blame, and Johnson would go away happy.

Lady Bird Johnson knocks and enters the bedroom and asks Jackie if she needs help changing. She declines the offer, then says, 'What if I had not been there? I'm so glad I was there.'

On the tarmac, Vernon Oneal has arrived to collect his white hearse. Over the next 12 months he will send Jackie Kennedy bills for the cost of the casket. The government finally pays him $3400, less than he wanted, because they believed he was deliberately exaggerating the casket's value.

2.20pm/3.20pm EST

Johnson's secretary has been patched through to Robert Kennedy at home in Virginia, and to the deputy attorney general Nick Katzenbach in the White House. She's poised to write down the wording of the oath of office. Robert Kennedy starts reading it, stops and then lets Katzenbach take over.

'I do solemnly swear, parenthesis, or affirm, parenthesis, that I will faithfully execute the, capital letter, Office of the President of the United States, comma, and will to the best of my ability, comma, preserve, comma, protect and defend the Constitution of the United States, period.'

2.25pm

In Room 317 in City Hall, Captain JW Fritz is asking Oswald where he went to school, and about his time in the Marine Corps. Fritz likes to get acquainted with suspects at the start of an interrogation. He's soft-spoken and has a reputation as a skilled interrogator. He's been so long in the job that he was part of the squad that hunted for Bonnie and Clyde in the 1930s. Fritz loves wearing cowboy hats – and all his detectives copy him. On the streets of Dallas, Fritz's men are easy to spot.

Henry Wade, the Dallas district attorney, thinks Fritz is the best man at solving a crime he ever saw, but he is the poorest at getting evidence. No one is transcribing what Oswald is saying. The Dallas Police Department has no recording devices, despite Fritz's repeated requests over the past six years. (The accounts that follow of what was said during Oswald's interrogations are based on the notes Fritz made a few days later and by others who were present.)

Johnson has asked press secretary Mac Kilduff to make sure there's press on board to witness the swearing in. Johnson spots White House photographer Cecil Stoughton.

'Where do you want us, Cecil?'

2.30pm

Six policemen are standing in front of the open front door to Ruth Paine's house. They ring the doorbell and Ruth comes out to the porch.

'We have Lee Oswald in custody. He's charged with shooting an officer,' says Detective Guy Rose, who's come straight from the interrogation room in City Hall. Ruth asks if they have a warrant. Rose says they haven't, but they can easily get one from a judge. Ruth lets the policemen in. Marina watches them in a cold sweat as they search the house.

2.34pm

Robert Oswald is on the expressway from Denton to Dallas, driving at top speed away from a car that he can see in his rear-view mirror is gaining on him. Could it be the FBI or has someone recognised him as Lee's brother? he wonders. The car draws level and Robert recognizes two executives from work. They wave at him to pull over.

2.36pm

Clint Hill has been summoned by Jackie to see her in the presidential cabin. He's asking what she needs. She takes both his hands.

'What's going to happen to you now, Mr Hill?'

His eyes fill with tears.

'I'll be okay, Mrs Kennedy. I'll be okay...'

Admiral Burkley is still sitting with the casket, his black medical bag with its now unnecessary medicines and spare sunglasses not far away. Dave Powers sits down next to him, as he has no desire to witness the swearing-in ceremony that's about to take place. Roy Kellerman can see agent Paul Landis is weeping.

'Pull yourself together, Paul. You're witnessing history. Come in here...'

On the plane, agent Dick Johnsen still has the bullet in his pocket.

On the side of the expressway, the two Acme bosses are asking if Robert would like them to go with him to Dallas. Robert's eyes fill with tears at their kindness, and he says that this is something he has to do alone. Before driving off, they give him $70.

2.38pm

Twenty-six people are squeezed in the small stateroom of Air Force One, where Lyndon B Johnson is about to be sworn in as the 36th president of the United States by his old friend Judge Sarah T Hughes, who's just been collected from the Trade Mart lunch and driven at high speed to Love Field. The blinds are still down and there's still no air conditioning. When Johnson walks in, it seems to his aides as if he's become a different man – somehow taller and more statesmanlike.

There is no sign of Jackie Kennedy, and Johnson is keen to have her in the official photograph.

'Do you want to ask Mrs Kennedy if she would like to stand with us?' he asks Kenny O'Donnell. O'Donnell doesn't move. Johnson glares at him, furious.

'She said she wants to be here when I take the oath. Why don't you see what's keeping her?' O'Donnell reluctantly heads towards Jackie's bedroom. UPI reporter Merriman Smith notes that when she arrives, Jackie is dry-eyed, but her face is 'a mask of shock'. Johnson takes her by the hand and guides her to stand next to him. Photographer Cecil Stoughton arranges the rest of the witnesses for an historic photograph.

Five years earlier, Johnson said to an aide, 'I do understand power, whatever else may be said about me, I know where to look for it, and how to use it.'

Johnson recites the oath of office. Standing on a sofa with

his back to the wall, Cecil Stoughton captures the scene. Johnson has his hand on JFK's Catholic missal (brought in haste from the bedroom, mistaken for a Bible); on his right side is Lady Bird, and on his left, Jackie, her hair falling across her face, still wearing her bloodstained pink suit (she had ignored the fresh clothes laid out for her by the Johnson staff).

Mac Kilduff is recording the occasion on a Dictaphone he'd found on JFK's desk on the plane. The ceremony lasts half a minute.

'Now let's get airborne!' Johnson calls out.

Chief Curry walks up to the former first lady.

'Mrs Kennedy, believe me. We did everything we possibly could...'

He then disembarks so he can get back to the Police Department at City Hall.

2.47pm

Air Force One is taxiing towards the runway; not far behind it is Air Force Two, now filled with Kennedy staffers, and behind that is a C130 cargo jet carrying the president's limousine.

Jackie Kennedy is seated next to her husband's casket. O'Donnell is with her.

'Oh, Kenny! What's going to happen...?'

'You want to know something Jackie? I don't give a damn,' he says.

Police officers are still searching Ruth Paine's house. Guy Rose is on the phone to Captain Fritz who tells him to ask Marina if her husband owns a rifle. Ruth immediately says 'no' then translates the question for Marina. Marina says something in Russian to Ruth, who, clearly shocked, says, 'Yes, he does have a rifle.'

Holding baby June, Marina leads the police to the garage where the Oswalds store their belongings. She points to the blanket on the floor. A policeman picks it up, and it hangs limp in his arms. There's nothing in it. Marina gasps. She knows now that her husband shot the president. Guy Rose thinks she's going to faint.

2.55pm

Having parked in the City Hall basement garage and managed to avoid the television crews setting up their equipment, FBI agent James Hosty is riding in a City Hall elevator with Lieutenant Jack Revill, a high-flier in Dallas law enforcement. The two men often work together, but don't get along. Revill has just come from the Book Depository and tells Hosty that they suspect a man named Lee is involved in the killing of the president.

'Jack, the Lee you are looking for is Lee Oswald. He killed Tippit! He's a communist and he probably killed Kennedy too. He's under arrest now upstairs!' Hosty says.

'Well, if you know that Oswald killed Kennedy, why the hell didn't you tell us? Why didn't you tell us that Oswald was in town and a known communist?'

'Jack, I couldn't tell you. You know Bureau policy – the "need to know rule".'

The FBI don't consider local police qualified to be part of a 'need to know' group.

Hosty heads off to Captain Fritz's office, and Revill to find a clerk to dictate a record of their conversation.

3.01pm/4.01pm EST

J Edgar Hoover is on the phone to Robert Kennedy saying that they have in custody the man they think killed his brother.

President Johnson is sitting in the stateroom of Air Force One. He takes one of its notepads embossed with the presidential seal, and writes his immediate priorities:

1. Staff
2. Cabinet
3. Leadership

Dave Powers is telling Roy Kellerman that Mrs Kennedy wants the autopsy done at Bethesda Naval Hospital, as her husband was in the Navy, and that she wants the agents to carry her husband's body from the plane, and Bill Greer to drive it to the hospital. She feels sorry for Greer, who is full of remorse, feeling that he should have swerved to avoid the final fatal shot.

> *Oswald was quite composed. He answered readily those questions that he wanted to answer. He could cut off just like with a knife anything that he didn't want to answer... He was not particularly obnoxious. He seemed to be intelligent. He seemed to be clear-minded... He talked with his hands all the time. He was handcuffed, but he was quiet... well, he was not what you call a stoic phlegmatic person. He was very definite with his talk and his eyes and his head...*
>
> **Harry Holmes testimony to the Warren Commission**
> **2nd April 1964**

3.10pm

The third floor of City Hall is in chaos. No one from the police is checking the credentials of the press – it's a free-for-all, reporters broadcasting live to the nation, photographers, large TV cameras, and even members of the public, all blocking the narrow seven-foot-wide corridor. TV technicians have hung cables from third-floor windows down to their trucks in the street below – some are even slung through Chief Curry's office. Adding a surreal touch to the scene, a teenage sailor in uniform is there, hoping to do a story for his high school newspaper.

Out-of-town journalists, not knowing who is who in Dallas law enforcement, are following the Dallas television and radio reporters around. Sympathetic cops are allowing some of the members of the press they know to use their office phones.

After the national embarrassment of UN Ambassador Adlai Stevenson being spat on and hit with a placard when he visited in October, the City of Dallas has hired a local public relations firm to advise the police on how to handle the press. The Sam Bloom Agency recommended that the police should be completely open. The chaos of the third floor is the result.

In Captain Fritz's office, James Hosty is introducing himself to Oswald and reading him his rights. He doesn't get very far.

'Oh, so you're Hosty – I've heard about you, you're the one who's been harassing my wife!' Oswald shouts. Hosty sees Fritz and the other officers exchange puzzled looks.

'My wife is a Russian citizen who is in this country legally and is protected under diplomatic laws from harassment by you or any other FBI agent! If you wanted to talk to me, you should have come directly to me, not my wife. You never responded to my request.'

To Hosty, those words sound familiar. On the 12th November someone had called in at the FBI office in Dallas and left an unsigned, misspelled note for 'Hasty', telling him to 'cease bothering my wife... if you have anything you want to learn about me, come talk to me directly'. Hosty had put it in his in-tray and forgotten about it until this moment. He deals with 40 cases at any one time, and had no idea who could have sent it.

Bob Schieffer from the *Star-Telegram* is driving to Dallas with Marguerite Oswald, and he's shocked by what she's saying.

'Everyone will feel sorry for his wife, but they won't feel sorry for me and she will get a lot of money and I won't get any and I'll starve to death...'

Her comments are so bizarre that Schieffer never puts them in his story that he files that night.

Fifty-six-year-old Marguerite has lived a turbulent, unsettled life, married three times and with three sons – John, Robert and Lee. The first two fled their controlling and money-obsessed mother as soon as they could. Marguerite spoilt Lee, tolerating his truancy from school and his violent temper. But in the end, he too had left her.

Schieffer never will work out why she rang for a lift, unless it was because she wanted to save money on a taxi.

3.15pm/4.15pm EST

Helen Markham, the waitress who witnessed the shooting of Officer Tippit, is in City Hall. She knows that any moment she may have to face the gunman in a line-up, and the prospect is making her ill. Detective Jim Leavelle reassures her that she won't be seen, and all she has to do is say the number over the head of the man she saw shoot the officer.

Fourteen-year-old Susan Cooke is standing by the front door of her parents' Fifth Avenue apartment in Manhattan. She's in her cheerleader uniform, as she'd expected to be at a basketball game and had walked home in a daze after hearing the news of the assassination from a teacher at school, who wept as she told her pupils. As she stands in the hall, she can hear that the radio and television are on, and that her father Alistair is on the phone. Cigarette smoke is pouring from his study. He's trying to find out what has happened in Dallas, so he can file his piece for the *Guardian*, and write his *Letter from America* for the BBC. He'd been invited by the White House to cover the trip to Texas, but had declined, as he was bored with Democratic politics.

3.20pm

Sergeant Joseph Ayres, the chief steward on Air Force One, is putting a call through from Lyndon Johnson to Rose Kennedy, the late president's mother.

'Mrs Kennedy, I have...' he falters, not wishing to upset her further by giving Johnson his new title, '...er, Mr Johnson for you here.'

'What do I say to her?' Johnson says to Ayres, covering the receiver with his hand.

'I wish to God there was something that I could do and I wanted to tell you that we are grieving with you,' Ayres replies.

Johnson takes his hand away.

'I wish to God there was something that I could do and I wanted to tell you that we are grieving with you...' he says.

It is clear from her terse reply that Rose can't wait to get off the phone.

Johnson then calls Nellie Connally at the Parkland Hospital. She tells him that her husband is making a remarkable recovery. He is now being guarded by a troop of armed Texas Rangers, ready to repel a second gunman if necessary.

The atmosphere on the plane continues to be tense. Johnson has twice asked to speak to Dave Powers and Kenny O'Donnell, but they've refused to leave Jackie and their dead president. When General Ted Clifton, JFK's military aide, had come into the rear compartment on a mission for Johnson, O'Donnell had snapped at him, 'Why don't you get back and serve your new boss?'

O'Donnell suspects that Johnson staged the oath-taking ceremony on board Air Force One, with Jackie by his side, so it looked to the world as if he had her blessing. Even the Texas accents of the new administration are irritating him.

Back in Dallas, Fritz, with his cowboy hat tilted back on his head, is questioning Oswald. Hosty is making notes.

'Did you win any medals for rifle shooting in the Marines?'

'Just the usual medals.'

'For what?'

'I got an award for marksmanship,' Oswald replies.

The news of the assassination has spread around the world. Speaking on the BBC, Prime Minister Sir Alec Douglas-Home said President Kennedy died 'when he bore on his shoulders all the cares and hopes of the world'. In the Soviet Union, radio and television programmes were interrupted and solemn organ music is being played. The mayor of West Berlin, Willie Brandt, declared, 'I feel as though a light has gone out, gone out for all men who hoped for peace and freedom and a better life.' He's asked Berliners to put a candle in their windows in tribute. President de Gaulle declared that JFK 'died like a soldier, under fire, for his duty and in the service of his country'. Chinese officials told US diplomats there will be no official message of sympathy from their leaders, as they have not been officially informed of the American president's death.

Liz Carpenter, Johnson's executive assistant, is writing a short address for her boss to give to the press and television cameras when they arrive at Andrews (she feared that the noise of a typewriter would seem inappropriate at a time like this). Carpenter is peering at some notes she'd made on the fast journey from Parkland Hospital, which are largely indecipherable.

For the last three years, all Johnson's speeches and statements had to be run past Kenny O'Donnell. This is the first that doesn't.

Forty thousand feet below her, every US Air Force base on their route is on red-alert; fighter pilots are sitting in their cockpits.

Seated by the casket of the dead president, Jackie, Kenny O'Donnell and Dave Powers are having what O'Donnell feels is a proper Irish wake, full of sentimental stories. Powers describes to Jackie her husband's last visit to his father Joe the previous month, and how on leaving he'd kissed his father's forehead, then returned to do it once more, as if he felt he'd never see him again.

O'Donnell tells her that when her husband visited the grave of their baby son Patrick that same weekend, he'd said, looking at the grave, 'He seems so alone here.'

'I'll bring them together now,' Jackie whispers.

She decides then and there to have Patrick's body moved to Arlington Cemetery, where Jack will be buried.

3.30pm

Wearing his usual snap-brim hat to pass off as a detective, Bob Schieffer boldly strides up to the first Dallas police officer he can see.

'I'm the one who brought Oswald's mother over. Is there any place we can put her so these reporters won't talk to her?'

The policeman shows Schieffer a small office close to the burglary squad, and asks if that will do. Schieffer tells him it will be perfect. For the next few hours Schieffer and ten other *Star-Telegram* reporters use the room to interview Marguerite Oswald, and a police phone to file their reports.

3.40pm

Fritz is asking Oswald why he took a gun to the Texas Theater.

'I felt like it.'

'You felt like it?'

'You know how boys are when they have a gun, they carry it.'

'Did you shoot Officer Tippit?'

'No, I didn't. The only law I violated was when I hit the officer in the show, and he hit me in the eye and I guess I deserved it...'

Ruth Paine is knocking on a neighbour's door hoping that they can babysit her two children while she and Marina go to the police station. Accompanying her is a policeman, clearly keeping an eye on her. Ruth doesn't like feeling like a suspect.

3.50pm

O'Donnell pours Jackie a Scotch, the first she's ever had. For the rest of her life its taste will remind her of the flight from Dallas.

4.00pm/5.00pm EST

Joe Kennedy has woken from his afternoon nap. He suffered a stroke two years ago and can no longer speak coherently. Rose is concerned that the news of his son's death will make his condition worse. Joe is expecting to watch the news, as he does every day, when he wakes from his sleep. He's now pointing at the television, and Ted, newly arrived from Washington, gets on his knees to plug it in. Surreptitiously he pulls the wires out of the back of the set. When no picture appears he says, 'We'll fix it in the morning.'

But Ted can tell that his father knows that something is seriously wrong.

Six-year-old Agatha Pozen is playing with Caroline Kennedy in the White House. Maud Shaw thought it would be better if Caroline was kept busy, and the girls had been so disappointed when their sleepover was cancelled. John Jr is playing with family friend and journalist Ben Bradlee and showing him a salute that Dave Powers taught him. No one can bring themselves to tell the children.

Governor Connally's Stetson, which he was holding in his lap when he was shot, has been retrieved by the Dallas Police and is hanging on a hat stand in Chief Curry's office. It is spattered with blood.

4.05pm

As Air Force One gets closer to Andrews Air Force Base, Admiral Burkley is concerned about Jackie being seen still in her stained clothes. Earlier Mac Kilduff had been shocked to see dried blood under her bracelet. The admiral is kneeling next to Jackie. 'Another dress?'

'No. Let them see what they've done.'

Lieutenant Jack Revill is dictating to a clerk an account of his conversation with Hosty. It ends with a sentence that will have lasting repercussions for the FBI and Hosty. Hosty will always deny saying it.

'Agent Hosty further stated that the FBI was aware of the Subject and that they had information that this Subject was capable of committing the assassination of President Kennedy.'

Kenny O'Donnell and Clint Hill are trying to decide whether Caroline and John Jr should be moved from the White House before their father's body arrives. They agree the children should stay with Jackie's mother Janet Auchincloss. Hill calls the White House.

4.10pm/5.10pm EST

Oswald, accompanied by three detectives, is heading for the elevator on his way to the identity parade. They're inching their way through the camera crews and the shouting reporters.

'Did you kill the president?'

'No, sir. Nobody charged me with that.'

Moments before, the police had searched him and discovered five .38 bullets in his pocket.

In the White House, Caroline and John Jr can hear a helicopter and are running to the window.

'Mommy and Daddy are coming home!' they shout.

Ben Bradlee says the first thing he can think of, 'Daddy will be back later...'

4.25pm

Reporter Travis Linn is back in the studios of WFAA and listening to the tape recording of the gunshots in Dealey Plaza. He's appalled – the portable recorder's tape has been bulk-erased and the reel-to-reel recorded over. But he remembers distinctly what he heard.

> *I asked them if they would turn him sideways. They did, and then they turned him back around, and I said 'The second', and they said, 'Which one?' and I said 'Number two'. So when I said that, well, I just kind of fell over.*
>
> **Helen Markham testimony to the Warren Commission**
> **26th March 1964**

Helen Markham is lying on the floor of the dark basement room in City Hall, where the identity parade has just taken place. She'd started to cry as soon as she saw Oswald led in, and as soon as she'd identified him, she'd fainted.

FBI agent James Hosty watched the line-up with satisfaction. They have the bastard who committed both murders, he's sure.

Marina and Ruth are in a police car heading to City Hall. Ruth Paine is looking out of the window, agonising about the fact that she got Lee the job at the Book Depository. He had seemed so ordinary. Marina suddenly asks her a question in Russian.

'Isn't it true that the penalty for shooting someone in Texas is the electric chair?'

'Yes, it's true...' Ruth replies.

On the plane, Kenny O'Donnell is remembering when President Kennedy left Shannon Airport on Air Force One that summer, and he'd seen a sign held up by someone in the waving crowd. It was the title of an old Irish song, 'Johnny, I Hardly Knew Ye'. It's seems particularly appropriate now.

4.45pm/5.45pm EST

The attorney general is sitting in the dark in the back of an empty Army truck at Andrews Air Force Base, waiting for his brother's body to arrive. Hiding from the television crews and their floodlights, he's thinking about the last time he'd been at this base waiting for Jack. It was October 1962, when a U-2 spy plane had confirmed the presence of Russian missile bases in Cuba, and the president had flown into Andrews from Chicago to deal with what would be the greatest crisis of the Cold War.

Janet Auchincloss, Jackie Kennedy's mother, is on the phone to Maud Shaw.

'We feel you should be the one to break the news to the children, at least to Caroline.'

'Oh no, please don't ask me to do that.'

'Please, Miss Shaw. It is for the best. They trust you... I am asking you as a friend... It has to be you.'

Miss Shaw stands silently for a few moments then says that she will tell Caroline when she puts her to bed that night.

4.58pm/5.58pm EST

The wheels of Air Force One, codename Angel, touch down at Andrews Air Force Base on the outskirts of Washington. Jackie says to Clint Hill, 'Let's remember the happy things, not the sad things.'

5.01pm/6.01pm EST

At Andrews, the TV crews turn off their floodlights so that Colonel Swindal can see his way to the plane's parking stand. Robert Kennedy takes advantage of the dark and jumps out of the Army truck and runs to the steps.

5.03pm/6.03pm EST

Robert Kennedy is running down the aisle towards the rear of Air Force One, his face streaked with tears. Johnson has his hand out to shake his, but the attorney general doesn't stop until he gets to Jackie. He hugs her, and then reaches out to touch the casket.

Secret Service agent Jeb Byrne, who had been guarding the president in Fort Worth, is mid-air on a flight to Washington. He's sobbing uncontrollably and the passengers on either side are looking alarmed.

'You will have to put up with this. I was in Texas with the president,' he tells them.

5.10pm/6.10pm EST

The TV floodlights are now back on, and cameras are broadcasting live pictures of a chaotic scene. A bright yellow truck, with a moveable platform designed to load meals onto military planes, is at the rear door of Air Force One. The handleless casket is being loaded onto it with difficulty by the Secret Service men, especially as the platform is two feet below the 707's rear door. Jackie and Robert and the rest of the Kennedy party jump onto it. After a short delay the platform drops jerkily towards the ground and the official military casket team run towards it. Their commanding officer Lieutenant Sam Bird watches with surprise as the Secret Service men and Kennedy aides push them away, wanting to be the ones to carry the casket to the waiting Navy ambulance. He wishes he'd brought a flag to cover the casket.

Robert Kennedy helps Jackie jump down from the truck, and they get into the back of the car. The waiting press and politicians can see the bloodstains on her skirt and tights.

Twenty yards from the plane, Nicholas Herbert of *The Times* is standing on the tarmac with other journalists and members of Kennedy's Cabinet. Herbert is shocked by the sight of blood on Jackie's dress, and looking around he can see hard-bitten colleagues in tears. Herbert met JFK at the White House in the early hours of the 21st January 1961 at the end of his inauguration day, and the president had remembered his name ever since.

He can see that the Secret Service agents are looking uneasy and tense. The floodlights illuminating Air Force One, and the crescent moon hanging in the dark sky, make the scene look even more dramatic. The smell of jet fuel and diesel oil fills the air.

Mac Kilduff had wanted to unload the casket from the other side of the plane, away from the cameras, but Jackie had vetoed it saying, 'We'll go out the regular way.' On Air Force One Johnson is fuming; he'd expected that he would escort Jackie off the plane.

In the ambulance are a nurse and a heart specialist, whom Roy Kellerman is now asking to leave, to make room for Admiral Burkley and the security detail. They've been sent by Lyndon

Johnson's doctor, who fears he might have another heart attack. As it is, there's still not much room, and Burkley has to sit on agent Paul Landis's lap. As the ambulance pulls away, President Johnson and Lady Bird are standing in the doorway of Air Force One, waiting for steps to arrive.

5.15pm/6.15pm EST

The new president, with Lady Bird next to him, is standing in front of a bank of microphones, holding the short statement Liz Carpenter had prepared for him on the plane. The sound of two helicopters about to take him and his aides to the White House is almost drowning his words.

'This is a sad time for all people. We have suffered a loss that cannot be weighed. For me it is a deep personal tragedy. I know the world shares the sorrow that Mrs Kennedy and her family bear. I will do my best. That is all I can do. I ask for your help – and God's.'

Nicholas Herbert and the other journalists have to confer when Johnson finishes, to check exactly what he said.

5.20pm/6.20pm EST

In his study overlooking Central Park, Alistair Cooke is typing fiercely. His piece for the *Guardian* is taking shape. Susan, his daughter, is working as his assistant, watching the television in the back room and switching between the networks so when there's a new development she can run into his study with the news. Susan is also giving him facts such as the name of Judge Sarah T Hughes, and pointing out mistakes in his copy. Her father is arguing on the phone with an impatient editor, 'Listen, we are doing the best we can!' Susan is filled with pride that he said 'we'.

5.23pm/6.23pm EST

The doctors have finished operating on Governor Connally.

'He's going to make it,' a medic tells Nellie.

'It was a nightmare scene at Andrews Air Force Base when the big blue and white presidential jet aircraft unloaded its gruesome cargo...'

Nicholas Herbert is dictating his copy to a *Times* shorthand writer in London, direct from the notes he'd scribbled standing on the tarmac. He has no time to write up anything more considered.

5.28pm/6.28pm EST

After a short helicopter ride, Lyndon Johnson is walking across the rose garden of the White House. By his side is agent Rufus Youngblood, who is so close, his shoulder keeps touching the president's. Behind them, a group of advisors stop when they reach the open French doors of the Oval Office. Johnson walks in alone.

During the Kennedy administration, he'd spent very little time in the Oval Office – only a matter of minutes with JFK in the past year. Denied any meaningful role as vice president, it was Robert Kennedy who was seen by many journalists as 'the Number 2 in Washington'.

'My future is behind me,' a miserable Johnson had told an aide that summer.

He looks at the new red carpet that Jackie had laid as a surprise for her husband on their return from Dallas.

Crowds are lining streets and bridges to see the ambulance make its way to Bethesda. Every so often Roy Kellerman sees

Bill Greer wipe his eyes. Jackie is talking to Robert over the casket, telling him about Dallas. Robert moves the ambulance's curtains aside and sees some children in pyjamas watching the motorcade.

Two Secret Service agents are at Jackie Kennedy's mother's house trying to fix Caroline's old cot so that John Jr can use it.

5.30pm

Nightclub owner Jack Ruby is at his sister Eva Grant's apartment, sitting in a chair and crying as he watches the television news.

'I never felt so bad in my life, even when Ma and Pa died... someone tore my heart out,' he says.

Jack loves his sister but they often bicker – when she calls his office he usually puts the receiver on the desk and lets her talk while he gets on with his work.

In 1947, Ruby came to Dallas to help Eva run her nightclub the Singapore Supper Club. He's always protected her – when they were growing up in Chicago if anyone picked on Eva he would track them down and beat them up.

Ruby's still a fighter. He once assaulted a musician in his club with brass knuckles, and had the tip of his left index finger bitten off in a scrap.

For the last two years, Ruby and Eva have run the Carousel Club – a strip joint in downtown Dallas. It needs no bouncer as Jack does his own enforcing. Whenever he throws a misbehaving 'punk' or 'character' out of the club, he shouts after them, 'This is a high-class place!'

He has a strong sense of right and wrong. When one of his strippers was given a black eye by her husband, the next time he came to the club Ruby beat him up and threw him down the stairs, despite the fact the girl was shouting 'Jack, I don't want you to hit him!'

Since childhood, Ruby has had a fear of being alone. For company he has numerous dachshunds back in his apartment (he calls them his children), and a lodger called George Senator who helps out at the Carousel.

Ruby can't be by himself – especially not on a day like this. He continues to weep as he and Eva watch the news. Ruby's mood isn't improved by the fact that he's been taking the diet drug Preludin as an upper, combined with the amphetamine Benzedrine.

5.55pm/ 6.55pm EST

Ruth Paine and Marina Oswald are making their way through the chaos that is the third floor of City Hall.

An honour guard of 200 sailors and a crowd of about 3,000 people are waiting outside Bethesda Naval Hospital for the ambulance. Clint Hill and Paul Landis lead Robert Kennedy and Jackie to the VIP suite on the 17th floor. It has a kitchen, a bedroom and a large drawing room. There they meet Robert's sister Jean, Jackie's mother Janet Auchincloss and stepfather Hugh, friends Ben and Toni Bradlee, and Charles and Martha Bartlett – the couple who had introduced 22-year-old Jackie to the young congressman 12 years before. Ben Bradlee thinks Jackie looks like a lost child.

'Oh, Jackie, if this had to happen, thank God he wasn't maimed,' says her mother.

Jackie says she intends to stay at the hospital until the autopsy is over. She's not going to leave the body of her dead husband.

Jack Ruby is crying on the phone to Bob Willis the drummer at the Carousel.

'What do you think of a character like that killing the president?'

'Jack, he's not normal; no normal man kills the president on his lunch hour and takes the bus home.'

'He killed our president. He killed our president...' Ruby sobs.

6.00pm/ 7.00pm EST

Jackie is shocked to hear that her children have been moved to her mother's house.

'They should be in their own beds. Mommy, my God, those poor children; their lives shouldn't be disrupted, now of all times!'

Clint Hill overhears, and realising that he and O'Donnell made the wrong decision on the plane, quickly calls Maud Shaw at the White House.

Lieutenant Sam Bird, in charge of the casket team representing each branch of the armed services, orders his eight men to guard the entrances to the morgue where the autopsy is about to take place.

6.15pm/7.15pm EST

Captain Fritz wants Marina to have a look at the rifle found in the Book Depository, so Lieutenant Carl Day is now carry-ing it above his head, through a crowd of stunned reporters. They take pictures and shout questions at him – which he ignores.

Robert's wife Ethel arrives at Bethesda. They embrace, and Ethel, who understands grief, as both her parents died eight years before in a plane crash, says she feels certain that Jack is in heaven 'showering graces down on us'.

'Oh, Ethel, I wish I could believe the way you do,' Jackie replies.

6.17pm

Marina is looking at the rifle. She says that it looks the same as Lee's – it has dark wood and a sight on it – but she's not sure.

She's terrified about what the police might ask next. She knows nothing about the shooting of the president, but she does know about Lee's attempt to kill General Walker. Marina's convinced that he can be executed even for attempted murder. She knows she won't be able to lie to the police.

6.20pm/7.20pm EST

Lyndon Johnson is at his desk in the Executive Office Building across the road from the White House. Behind him is an old presidential flag that one of his assistants has found in the basement.

Johnson is writing letters to Caroline and John Jr. He tells them that he shares their grief and that their father was a wise and devoted man. They are the first letters of his presidency.

6.25pm

On his way to the Shearith Israel Synagogue to pray for the dead president, Jack Ruby has stopped off at City Hall. He's always been a friend to the police, giving them free entry to his clubs, and even once wading in, fists flying, to help two outnumbered cops being beaten up. Ruby thinks that having policemen in his club gives it class. Everyone knows him at City Hall as a harmless attention-seeker who loves to be in the middle of any Dallas drama, so Ruby's found it easy to make his way up to the Police Department.

WFAA radio reporter Victor Robinson is standing in the third-floor corridor and is watching Ruby with his hand on the doorknob of Captain Fritz's office, starting to push it open.

'You can't go in there, Jack,' a policemen standing guard outside says.

Ruby makes a joke that Robinson can't hear, and heads out of sight.

6.30pm/7.30pm EST

In Lyndon Johnson's office, workmen arrive to install a hotline to Moscow.

Around 24 people are in the morgue of Bethesda Naval Hospital, as the autopsy of JFK begins. Autopsy pathologists Dr James Humes and Dr J Thornton Boswell, with the help of Kellerman, Greer and two FBI agents, lift the body out of the casket. Humes thinks that he has never seen more shocked or distressed people. He is also taken aback by what he's looking at on the autopsy table. The body is wrapped in sheets and the head is heavily bound with bloody bandages and gauze. The hands are clenched in fists, the eyes and mouth open. JFK's military aide General McHugh feels faint at the sight and heads for a bench. Roy Kellerman sits next to him to see if he's okay.

Before the autopsy begins, Humes asks for photographs and X-rays to be taken, to help the search for any bullets still inside the body.

6.56pm/7.56pm EST

Caroline, John Jr, Maud Shaw and their armed Secret Service escort are driving into the White House past a crowd of onlookers.

'What are all those people there for?' asks Caroline.

'To see you,' Maud Shaw replies. Back at their grandmother's house, the repaired crib is on its way back to the attic.

In New York, the stores along Fifth Avenue are turning off the lights in their Christmas window displays. At Saks Fifth Avenue the mannequins are being carried away and a large photograph of President Kennedy put in their place. The illuminated advertisements in Time Square have been turned off and the cinemas and theatres are all closed. Broadway is dark. One production due to open in four days, called *The Plot to Assassinate the Chase Manhattan Bank* will change its name to *The Plot Against the Chase Manhattan Bank*.

'I'm just a patsy!'

7.10pm/8.10pm EST

In Captain Fritz's office, Judge David L Johnston is charging Lee Harvey Oswald with murder, that he 'unlawfully, voluntarily, and with malice aforethought killed JD Tippit by shooting him with a gun'. Oswald interrupts.

'This isn't an arraignment. This isn't a court. How do I know this is a judge?'

'Shut up and listen!' Assistant District Attorney Bill Alexander snaps back. He's amazed at how calm and cocky Oswald is. An infantry captain in the Second World War, Alexander is well known in Dallas as a tough prosecutor who loves nothing better than taking part in a raid or an arrest with a .308 automatic in his belt. Oswald's smug attitude angers him so much he has to leave the room to stop himself punching him.

Robert Oswald is standing in City Hall with a policeman, waiting for an elevator to go up to the third floor. He puts his hand in his back pocket to get a handkerchief, and the officer suddenly turns to face him, bracing himself. Robert freezes, realising that the officer thinks he's pulling a gun. Very, very slowly, he produces the handkerchief, and the officer relaxes.

Dave Powers and Kenny O'Donnell are at Gawler's Funeral Home in Washington, choosing a casket for the burial, the other being too damaged for a state funeral. Piped music plays in the background. Gawler's looked after the arrangements for Presidents Taft and Franklin D Roosevelt.

As they look at the caskets, Powers says, 'In Charlestown where I grew up, they measured your importance by the prestige of the people who came to your funeral. I always thought that my funeral would be great because President Kennedy would come to it. And now here I am, helping to pick out his casket...'

7.15pm/8.15pm EST

The president's limousine has arrived by plane from Love Field and is being driven to the White House garage by agent Sam Kinney. The bubbletop is on and it's trapping a hideous smell. Kinney can't bear to look in the mirror at the car's empty, bloody back seat.

Robert Oswald has found his mother, who is in a room in the Police Department with two FBI agents called Brown, as well

123

as Bob Schieffer of the Fort Worth *Star-Telegram*. Marguerite interrupts the FBI men to say she wants to speak to her son alone. One of the Browns finds them an empty room.

'This room is bugged. Be careful what you say,' Marguerite warns.

'Listen, I don't care whether the room is bugged or not. I'd be perfectly willing to say anything I've got to say right here in the doorway. If you know anything at all about what happened, I want to know it right now. I don't want to hear any whys, ifs, or wherefores,' Robert says.

Marguerite says that she's convinced that Lee is working for the CIA and has been for many years. As she talks, Robert can see that far from being upset at her son's arrest, his mother is enjoying the limelight. She's always sought attention and now she has it – on a global scale.

Robert Kennedy is telling Jackie that the police think they've found her husband's killer and he says he's a communist. She's stunned.

'He didn't even have the satisfaction of being killed for civil rights. It had to be some silly little communist.'

7.30pm/8.30pm EST

It's bathtime, and Maud Shaw is finding it hard to pretend to be happy. She has to leave the children for a moment and looks out over Pennsylvania Avenue at the crowds gathered there.

Secretary of State for Defense Robert McNamara is sitting on the floor of the kitchen of the Bethesda Hospital suite while Jackie, sitting on a stool, is telling him everything about the shooting in Dallas. She's been talking for over an hour. To McNamara it seems as if she's trying to purge herself of the experience, to unburden her soul. Robert Kennedy listens, not saying anything.

7.45pm/8.45pm EST

Maud Shaw has said prayers with John Jr, tucked him in and is now reading a story to Caroline, whom she's looked after since she was 11 days old. After a while Maud can't see the page for tears. In August she had to tell Caroline about the death of baby Patrick. This is going to be so much harder.

'What's the matter, Miss Shaw? Why are you crying?' Caroline asks. Her nanny takes her in her arms.

'I can't help crying, Caroline, because I have some very sad news to tell you...' Maud Shaw would write in her memoirs of that moment, 'It was a dreadful time for us both.'

FBI agent James Hosty is in Gordon Shanklin's office. His supervisor is smoking, with ash down his front as usual. He holds up the 'Hasty' note from Oswald.

'What the hell is this?'

'It's no big deal, just your typical guff.'

'What do you mean, "typical guff"? The note was written by Oswald, the probable assassin of the president, and Oswald brought it into *this* office just ten days ago!'

'What's the big deal? So what if Oswald wrote this note and left it for me? What does that have to do with anything?' Hosty replies.

'If people learn that Oswald gave you guff a week before the assassination, they'll say you should have known he'd kill the president!'

Hosty says that if they explain the background to the note, then people will understand that he had no idea that Oswald was a potential assassin. Shanklin is not convinced.

I believed at that time, and I still believe it was a commu-nist activity, and I felt like there hadn't been more than one eyewitness, and if it got to be a known fact that I was an eyewitness, my family or I, either one, might not be safe.

Howard Brennan testimony to the Warren Commission
24th March 1964

7.50pm

Another line-up is taking place in the basement of City Hall. It consists of a jail clerk, two prisoners and Oswald. Construction worker Howard Brennan, who had a good view of the gunman on the sixth floor of the Book Depository, has lost his bravado of six hours before. He really doesn't want to be here.

Brennan's been talking it over with his wife all afternoon, and he's convinced that the assassination is part of a plot and that if he's the only witness, he and his family are in great danger.

Oswald comes into the room and Brennan recognises him straightaway, but says to Secret Service agent Sorrels that although he looks most like the man he saw, he can't make a positive identification. Brennan, feeling guilty, reassures himself that Oswald will be arrested for the murder of Officer Tippit anyway, so his inconclusive evidence won't matter in the end.

Also looking at the line-up are sisters-in-law Barbara and Virginia Davis, who saw a man run across their lawn after the Tippit murder. Barbara looks at the men in the line-up, and recognises the person she saw.

'That's him,' Barbara says, pointing at Oswald. Virginia agrees.

8.15pm

Oswald is being led back once more through the crowd of reporters on the third floor.

'They're taking me in because of the fact I visited the Soviet Union. I'm just a patsy!'

8.20pm/9.20pm EST

Sargent Shriver, the husband of JFK's sister Eunice, has been working for over two hours preparing the large East Room of the White House for the casket. He has heard from Air Force One that Jackie wants President Lincoln's funeral to be the template for how her husband's should be. His guide is an engraving showing the East Room in 1865 when Lincoln's body lay there. (The engraving was found earlier that evening in a dark government warehouse by David Mearns, the director of the Library of Congress. The lights there operate on a timer and only work when the Library is open, so he had a difficult search using a torch.)

No one can find the catafalque Lincoln's coffin rested on (it'll soon be found in the basement of the Capitol), so White House carpenters are hastily making a replica.

The Lincoln engraving shows a room draped in yards of black cloth, but the White House didn't have any. Someone suggested black upholsterer's webbing used for the underside of chairs, and so they had contacted local upholsterers until they found one with enough material.

8.30pm/9.30pm EST

At Bethesda, the pathologists are examining an oval-shaped bullet wound just above the president's right shoulder blade.

They can see that the edges are pushed inward, consistent with an entrance wound. But they are perplexed by the absence of an exit wound, not realising that the tracheotomy performed eight hours earlier at Parkland had obliterated any evidence of it. (Dr Humes will speak to Dr Perry at Parkland on the phone the following day and be told about the tracheotomy.)

The evidence from the large head wound is clearer – it is a textbook example of an entrance and exit wound. The hole at the back of the skull has an edge that bevels inwards. The president was shot twice from behind, they conclude. The second bullet fragmented in his head.

President Johnson is at home, talking to his aides. The television is showing scenes from Fort Worth that morning. He lifts his hand to shield his eyes from the screen.

'I don't believe I can take that. It's too fresh,' he says.

Johnson then calls James J Rowley, the head of the Secret Service, and praises Rufus Youngblood's bravery in Dallas.

'I want you to do whatever you can, the best thing that can be done for that boy.'

8.40pm/9.40pm EST

Maud Shaw is in her room between Caroline's and John Jr's. She is trying to knit, but her hands aren't steady enough.

Every half-hour or so, Clint Hill is phoning down to Roy Kellerman in the morgue to find out when they can leave with the body.

Robert Kennedy is on the phone speaking to Marie Tippit. He offers her his deepest sympathies and says that if his brother hadn't come to Dallas her husband would still be alive.

'But you know, they got killed doing their jobs. He was being the president and JD was being the policeman he was supposed to be,' Marie replies.

In two weeks' time, Marie will receive a gold-framed photo of John F Kennedy and his family, with a message from Jackie written underneath.

'For Mrs JD Tippit – with my deepest sympathy and the knowledge that you and I now share another bond – reminding our children all their lives what brave men their fathers were. With all my wishes for your happiness, Jacqueline Kennedy.'

8.50pm

Marguerite Oswald is in tears as she hugs her daughter-in-law. Robert is stunned to see that Marina is holding a baby – Lee hadn't told him that they had a second child. Before he can say anything, Ruth Paine introduces herself.

'I'm a friend of Marina and Lee. I'm here because I speak Russian, and I'm interpreting for Marina.'

She introduces her husband Michael, explaining that they are no longer living together. Robert can see that, like his mother, Ruth Paine is loving the attention.

'Oh, Mrs Oswald, I am so glad to meet you! Marina has often expressed the desire to contact you, especially after the baby was born. But Lee didn't want her to.'

'Mrs Paine, you speak English. Why didn't *you* contact me?' Marguerite snaps.

9.00pm/10pm EST

Special agent Jerry Blaine is part of the White House detail, and is at home in Washington writing his daily report. He says that his agents are suffering from 'acute guilt and failure' and that in the coming weeks they will become the scapegoat for what happened in Dealey Plaza. What makes it harder is that they not only lost a president, he writes, 'we lost a personal friend...'

9.05pm

Oswald is watching Sergeant Pete Barnes getting his equipment ready to make a paraffin cast of his hands, hoping to capture gunpowder residue.

'What are you trying to do, prove that I fired a gun?" Oswald says.

'I am not trying to prove that you fired a gun. We have the test to make, and the chemical people at the city-county laboratory will determine the rest of it.'

9.15pm

Abraham Zapruder is driving around Dallas trying to come to terms with what he filmed that afternoon.

9.20pm

Captain Fritz and Assistant District Attorney Bill Alexander are in the Majestic Steak House over the road from City Hall, discussing the case over steaks and coffee, trying to decide if they have enough evidence to charge Oswald with the murder of President Kennedy. It's looking as if they have, but Fritz wants to wait for fingerprint and firearm evidence first.

Bill Alexander decides that when he gets back to the office, for the first time in his 15-year career, he's going after some publicity.

9.30pm

Pete Barnes is walking though the reporters trying to get the casts to his fourth-floor office. They are shouting at him, 'What have you got in that sack, what have you got in that sack? You owe it to the news media to give it to us! What have you got in that sack?'

9.45pm

Marina, Marguerite and the Paines have been driven home by the police. Now *Life* magazine reporter Tommy Thompson and photographer Allan Grant are watching as Marguerite and Ruth Paine argue. The men had arrived unannounced a few moments before and begun to ask questions and take photographs. Now Mrs Oswald insists that they should be paid if they're going to appear in *Life*.

'Here is my daughter-in-law with two small children, and I, myself, am penniless, and if we are going to give this information, I believe we should get paid for it.'

Ruth says that Marina should be allowed to speak to the reporters. Marguerite is convinced that Ruth Paine set the whole thing up and got paid for it.

'I'm his mother! I'm the one who's going to speak!' Marguerite shrieks.

Thompson says he will call his office and see what they say about payment; Grant continues to take pictures.

George Carter of the *Dallas Times Herald* is asking Assistant District Attorney Bill Alexander when he's going to charge Oswald.

'As soon as I can draw up the complaint.'

'For what?'

'Murder.'

'How will it read?'

'Did then and there voluntarily and with malice aforethought kill John F Kennedy by shooting him with a gun in furtherance of a communist conspiracy.'

Alexander knows that he can't legally word it like that, but he's sick of all the talk in the media about Dallas right-wingers. Alexander has no evidence of a plot, but he knows Oswald was a communist, having seen left-wing literature when he searched his room personally in Beckley that afternoon.

Part of Alexander's job, as he sees it, is to protect the image of Dallas.

10.00pm/11.00pm EST

Bill Alexander isn't done yet. Joe Goulden of the *Philadelphia Inquirer,* who had dealings with Alexander when he was a reporter in Dallas, is on the phone asking what's going on.

'We're not getting anything straight. Is Oswald going to be charged with killing the president?'

'Yeah, we're getting ready to file on the communist son of a bitch.'

The doctors conducting the autopsy at Bethesda have spent a lot of time trying to find the first bullet, which they believe must still be inside the president's body. But FBI agent Jim Sibert has solved the mystery. He's just phoned the FBI firearms laboratory to see if there is such a thing as a bullet that could completely disintegrate and disappear. An agent at the lab says that he hasn't heard of such a thing, but did Sibert know that a bullet had been found on a stretcher at Parkland Hospital and handed to a Secret Service agent? Sibert heads off to tell the doctors at Bethesda their search is over.

10.10pm/11.10pm EST

Janet Auchincloss is knocking on Maud Shaw's door. She's concerned that John Jr will run into their father's room in the morning and expect him there.

'Tell the children that Uncle Coo (their step-grandfather) and I will be in the president's room.'

10.15pm

Jack Ruby shut his two clubs this afternoon out of respect for the president. He's now driving around Dallas to see whether his competitors have done the same. Ruby has been crying most of the afternoon over the loss of a man he thinks was the greatest that ever lived. His favourite dachshund Sheba (he jokingly calls her his wife) is sitting in the back seat. In his pocket is a .38 calibre Colt Cobra pistol. Earlier he'd taken it out and left it in the trunk of his car when he'd visited the Shearith Israel Synagogue to pray for the dead president. The rabbi, Hillel Silverman, thought that Ruby looked to be in a state of shock.

10.30pm

With Marguerite Oswald gone from City Hall, Bob Schieffer's luck is about to run out. For hours the Fort Worth *Star-Telegram* reporter had been using a police interview room to talk to Marguerite, and a police phone to file his stories, but an FBI agent has become suspicious. He asks Schieffer who he works for, and when he admits he's a reporter the agent says, 'I'm going to kill you if I ever see you again.' Schieffer heads speedily back to Fort Worth, angry that he never got an interview with Lee Harvey Oswald.

Life magazine reporter Tommy Thompson and photographer Allan Grant are in a car outside Ruth Paine's house. Thompson wants to make sure that no one else arrives to spoil their scoop.

Inside, Ruth and Marina are in the kitchen eating hamburgers Ruth's husband Michael got for them from a drive-thru. Marina tells Ruth that Lee had told her yesterday that he wanted them to get an apartment together. Ruth can see that she's hurt and confused, as if she was wondering how he could have said such a thing when he was planning to kill the president. Ruth has to ask the question:
 'Do you think that Lee killed the president?'
 'I don't know,' Marina replies, ending the conversation.

Ruth's house has only two bedrooms, so Marguerite is getting ready for a night on the couch.

10.45pm/11.45pm EST

The television is on in the bedroom of the Bethesda Hospital suite, showing montages of Kennedy's life, and footage from earlier that day. No one is watching, but no one is prepared to turn it off.

District Attorney Henry Wade has just finished dinner with his wife and is listening to the radio. A reporter says that Oswald is to be charged as part of 'an international communist conspiracy'. Wade is incredulous; no such crime exists in Texas – only murder with malice. He suspects that someone in City Hall is using the press for their own agenda. Wade has the law in his blood. The son of a judge, five of his brothers are lawyers. He is ambitious and not afraid of the limelight.

His phone rings and it's Waggoner Carr, the attorney general for the State of Texas, who's had a call from the White House concerned about the report of a conspiracy.

'This would be a bad situation, if you allege this is part of a Russian conspiracy, and it may affect international relations...'

Wade heads down to City Hall to see what's going on.

10.50pm

Robert Oswald is checking into the Statler-Hilton Hotel. A policeman said that it was okay for him to go.

'You seem a regular guy who's just gotten dragged into this mess.'

Oswald thinks about registering under a pseudonym, but decides not to hide his identity. In the end, the name Oswald means nothing to the receptionist nor to the bellhop who takes him to his room.

Dallas FBI agent Vincent Drain has been given the urgent task of taking Oswald's rifle and other key evidence to Washington for tests. To his horror he's just found out that there are no more flights out of Dallas to the capital that night. In desperation he's calling a general he knows at Carswell Air Force Base, to see if he can arrange a plane for him.

11.00pm

In her bedroom at the Paines' house, Marina Oswald is leafing through June's baby book. In it she finds the two photographs taken in their backyard showing Lee dressed in black and holding the rifle. She takes them to show her mother-in-law.

'Oh, no!' Marguerite says, and signals that Ruth should not know about this.

11.05pm/12.05pm EST

The Chicago FBI is banging on the door of William J Waldman. They believe the Mannlicher-Carcano rifle may have been sold to Oswald by Waldman's company, Klein's Sporting Goods.

Lying in the president's four-poster, Janet Auchincloss cannot sleep. The combination of its horsehair mattress and wooden board underneath is unbearable. She knew her son-in-law suffered with his back during the day, but never imagined he had to put up with this at night.

11.10pm

Marina has made another discovery. On the bureau in her bedroom, in the little china cup that belonged to her grand-mother, she's found Lee's wedding ring. Her heart sinks. He never took off his ring, not even for the dirtiest jobs.

That night she doesn't sleep; all she can see when she closes her eyes is the electric chair.

11.50pm

Chief Curry, Captain Fritz and District Attorney Wade are in the third-floor corridor, surrounded by reporters. He's just announced that Oswald has been charged with President Kennedy's murder. He faces a barrage of questions.

'Was there any indication that this was an organised plot or was there just one man?'

'We... there's no one else but him.'

'Mr Wade, could you elaborate on the physical evidence?'

'Well, we've gone on some other things that were gathered, the gun is one of them.'

'Are you going to bring him out?'

'Could we get a room where we could get a picture of him?'

'Can we get a press conference where he could stand against a wall and we could talk to him?'

'Will there be a way to take any pictures?'

'I don't see any reason to take any picture of him,' Wade says.

'Of Lee?'

'Yes.'

'Well, the whole world's waiting to see what he looks like,' a reporter says.

'Oh is that all? The whole world...' replies Wade, sarcastically.

1.33pm Friday 22nd November: Acting Press Secretary Malcolm 'Mac' Kilduff announces the death of President Kennedy.

Saturday 23rd November 1963

12.00am

KRLD radio presenter Jay Hogan is reading his last live bulletin of the day. He's decided to end it with something special – a poem he's been working on for the last hour.

'Mr President, may we say one last goodnight,
Where there must be perpetual light
In your faraway Valhalla, wherever,
Reserved for souls like yours.
And we can still see your bright smile
And your vigorous stride
Through some mystic Elysian fields
Good night, Mr President – good night.'

00.05am

'If anything goes wrong with his being down here, if there's a rush... he's immediately going out and that's it. Now do we understand each other?'

Chief Curry is briefing the reporters and TV crews squeezed into the police line-up room. It's so full even Captain Fritz can't get in. There's a small stage at the front and Fritz wanted Oswald on it in case someone attacked him, but Curry refused, so he'll stand just in front of the stage. Nobody has checked the ID of the people in the room. At the back, standing on a table, is Jack Ruby with his loaded revolver in his belt.

> *I said to this policeman, 'What's happening?' and he said, 'Well, actually there's a press conference down here,' pointing to a flight of steps into the basement of the building – 'there's a press conference in here in a few minutes.' And I said, 'Well, actually I'm from the Liverpool Echo and this is my photographer,' and we went down there. It's a story that I've told so often that you get to the point where you don't really believe it yourself, it just seems so unlikely...*
>
> **John Peel interview 23rd June 1996**

A few feet away from Ruby, John Ravenscroft is also waiting for the arrival of Oswald, having pretended once more to be a reporter from the *Liverpool Echo,* and that his mate Bob is a photographer. The fact that they didn't have a notebook or a camera went unnoticed. Earlier, his girlfriend Nancy told him when Kennedy's death was announced by her school principal, some of the students had cheered at the news.

00.08am/1.08am EST

Special agent Jerry Blaine is in Spring Valley, Washington DC, on duty outside the back door of President Johnson's house. He's armed with the regulation .38 calibre revolver, but also tonight with a Thompson submachine gun. No one is sure whether Oswald is part of a wider conspiracy. Blaine is exhausted after the Texas trip.

Suddenly he can hear someone approaching from a clockwise direction – a Kennedy agent would never approach that way. He pulls the bolt on top of the Thompson and lifts it to his shoulder. He has his finger on the trigger when the new president of the United States appears through the gloom. Lyndon Johnson turns white at the sight of the machine gun pointed at his chest. Blaine apologises.

In the morning Johnson will be briefed about the Secret Service 'counterclockwise movement' protocol.

00.10am

Live pictures are being broadcast of two detectives leading Lee Harvey Oswald into the police line-up room. About one hundred people are in there. Oswald is wearing a brown shirt over a white T-shirt and he has a cut over his right eye and a swollen left eyelid from his scuffle with Officer McDonald.

Jack Ruby is watching Oswald closely and thinks he looks proud of what he's done. Oswald then lifts his handcuffed hands over his head; to Ruby it's a triumphant clenched-fist communist salute.

Flashbulbs pop and questions are fired from reporters just a couple of feet from Oswald. He's calm and starts to answer, but is drowned out by reporters at the back shouting, 'Louder! Louder! Down in front!'

'Did you kill the president?

'No, I have not been charged with that. In fact no one has said that to me yet. Er, the first thing I heard about it was when the newspaper reporters in the hall asked me that question.'

'You *have* been charged,' Bob Mercer of KRLD radio says.

'Sir?' Oswald replies, leaning forward.

'Nobody said what?! Nobody said what?!' a frustrated reporter shouts.

'You *have* been charged,' Mercer says again. Oswald purses his lips and for the first time looks flustered. Chief Curry thinks the press are edging too close to Oswald and says, 'Okay, okay' to his detectives and Oswald is led out.

'What did you do in Russia?'

'How did you hurt your eye?'

Oswald leans into the reporter's microphone,

'A policeman hit me...'

The press at the back of the room shout to their colleagues at the front asking what Oswald said.

John Ravenscroft thinks Oswald's bewilderment looks convincing, and he's either innocent or a very good actor.

For Bob Mercer of KRLD, when Oswald left the room there was a feeling like air being sucked from the atmosphere after an explosion.

00.20am

Oswald is now in maximum security cell F-2 on the fifth floor. Two guards have been posted outside on suicide watch.

00.40am

FBI agent Vincent Drain's call to his friend at Carswell worked. When he got to the base 20 minutes earlier there was an empty Boeing KC 135 Stratotanker waiting to take him to Washington. Now he's climbing the steps to the plane with his precious packages: the Mannlicher-Carcano rifle found in the Book Depository; the paper sack and two spent shells found by the window (the third is in Chief Curry's drawer); a live 6.5 millimetre shell found in the rifle; the blanket found in Ruth Paine's garage; a shirt of Oswald's and his .38 revolver; a fragment of the bullet found in Governor Connally's wrist and a bullet removed from the body of Officer Tippit.

1.00am/2.00am EST

Kenny O'Donnell is in the morgue talking to Admiral Burkley. He wants to return the wedding ring that Jackie put on JFK's finger 12 hours before. Burkley works the ring free, and takes it to give to Jackie himself.

Outside the line-up room, Jack Ruby is talking to Judge David L Johnston.

'Come by and see me sometime at my club.'

He gives him a pass to the Carousel. It has a picture of a naked girl in black stockings holding a champagne glass.

Oswald has been taken to the Identification Bureau on the fourth floor. He's posed for mugshots – front and profile – and is now being fingerprinted. But he deliberately drags his inky fingers across the card instead of rolling them, forcing the policeman to take his fingers one by one and do it properly. He's asked to sign the bottom of the fingerprint card, but he refuses.

1.10am

District Attorney Wade is taking questions from reporters.

'Is he a member of any communist-front organisation?'

'That I can't say at the present time.'

'Any organisations that he belongs to that you know of?'

'The only one mentioned was the Free Cuba movement or whatever...'

'Fair Play for Cuba,' Jack Ruby shouts from the back of the room, correcting Wade.

'Out of the depths I cry to you, O Lord.'

1.20am

On the flight deck of the KC 135 Stratotanker, Vincent Drain is sitting with the pilot and co-pilot. They're listening to the shortwave broadcasts by the British, French and Canadian navies, as their ships and submarines put to sea in case of a Russian attack.

In his cell, Oswald is lying on his bunk, his shoes kicked off, eyes closed, hands clasped behind his head. His breathing is slow but the guards outside can't tell for sure he's asleep.

Ike Pappas of WNEW-News had managed to get a flight out of New York and he'd joined the throng of reporters shouting questions at Oswald in the shambolic midnight press conference. Now he's standing by a public phone looking around frantically because his New York office want him to get an interview with District Attorney Henry Wade. A small man in a pinstriped blue suit and fedora comes up to him.

'What's the matter?' he asks.

'I'm looking for Henry Wade.'

'What are you, a reporter?'

'Yeah. Are you a cop?' says Pappas, hoping this guy has an office and phone he can use.

'No, my name is Jack Ruby. I run the Carousel Club.' He gives him his card.

'Do you want Henry Wade? Hold on...'

Ruby walks over to Wade, who looks over at Pappas and says, 'Tell him I'll be right there.'

1.30am/2.30pm EST

In the Bethesda morgue, Joseph Hagan of Gawler's Funeral Home is looking at the body of the dead president. He snips off a locket of hair and says to his assistant, 'Go back to the funeral home and match this. Bring enough hair to cover this open section on the head.'

1.35am

Judge David L Johnston is advising Lee Harvey Oswald of his right to remain silent, and then reading complaint number F-154: 'that he did unlawfully, voluntarily and with malice aforethought kill John F Kennedy by shooting him with a gun against the peace and dignity of the State.'

'I don't know what you're talking about. That's the deal, is it?' Oswald says.

1.45am/2.45am EST

In the kitchen of the 17th-floor suite at Bethesda, Jackie is talking with Bob McNamara and Robert Kennedy. She's insisting on a closed casket.

'It's the most awful morbid thing; they have to remember Jack alive.' The attorney general, perched on the fridge, says that the funeral will be a public event, not a private one. Jackie reluctantly gives in.

1.50am

Jack Ruby is in the offices of radio station KLIF. The staff know him well – he's constantly trying to get them to advertise his strip clubs. They always refuse, pointing out that their audience is mostly teenagers. Tonight Ruby has come with a bag full of corned-beef sandwiches and Cokes for them. Proud to have seen Oswald at close hand, he's telling producer Glenn Duncan that Oswald could pass himself off as a college student and has the looks of the actor Paul Newman.

2.00am/3.00am EST

Admiral Burkley is handing the ring to Jackie. She tells him how much his care had meant to her and her husband. She reaches into her jacket pocket and gives him one of the red rose petals that he had given her in the back of the Oneal hearse.

'This is the greatest treasure of my life,' he says.

President Johnson is sitting up in bed, wearing a pair of striped pyjamas. Around his bed are seated aides and advisors. Lady Bird is asleep in another room. Johnson has been talking non-stop about his plans for the next few weeks, but now wraps things up.

'Well, goodnight, boys. Get a lot of sleep fast. It's going to be a long day tomorrow.'

Chief of Homicide and Robbery, Captain Will Fritz, sends his men home; he too needs his team as fresh as possible in the morning.

2.45am/3.45am EST

To Clint Hill it looks as if Jack Kennedy is sleeping. The dead president is lying on the autopsy table, naked and covered in a white sheet. Hill has been asked by Roy Kellerman to look at the body so that if Mrs Kennedy has any questions about it, he can answer them.

A doctor lowers the sheet and Hill is shown the wound in the throat, the wound at the top of the back that the doctor says is the entry wound, then the massive damage done by an explosive reaction in the head caused by a second bullet. Hill tells the doctor he knows full well what happened, as he was only five feet away. All he can think is that he should've got to the president in time to stop those bullets.

'If only I'd run faster...'

> *I am up there in the composing room talking to a guy by the name of Pat (sic) Gadash. He was so elated that I brought him this twist board, and I had it sealed in a polyethylene bag, but he wanted to see how it... worked. It is a board that is on a pivot, a ball bearing, and it has a tendency to give you certain exercises in twisting your body. So not that I wanted to get in with the hilarity of frolicking, but he asked me to show him, and the other men gathered around... I know you look like you are having a gay time, because naturally if your body is so free of moving, it is going to look that way. You follow me, gentlemen, as I describe it?*
> *Chief Justice Warren: Yes, I do.*
>
> *Jack Ruby testimony to the Warren Commission*
> *7th June 1964*

2.50am/3.50am EST

Jack Ruby is in the offices of the *Dallas Times Herald* to put in an ad saying his clubs will be closed on Saturday and Sunday night and to deliver a twist board to printer Clyde Gadash; it's an exercise device he's bought several dozen of, which he hopes will make him money. After ranting about the black-bordered ad in the *Morning News* the previous day, and weeping once more for Jackie and the kids, Ruby reluctantly shows the *Times Herald* staff how the twist board works, but his heart isn't in it.

A busload of Marines, who moments earlier had been asleep in their bunks, are getting into their uniforms as they're driven through the streets of Washington to the White House. Sargent Shriver had realised to his horror that there was no honour guard at the White House for the dead president, and so the order had gone out to summon the Marines based at nearby Fort Myer.

2.50am/2.50am EST

In a car park next to the attendant's hut not far from the Carousel Club, policeman Harry Olsen is sitting in his car drinking beer with one of Jack's strippers, an English girl called Kathy Kay. They met at the Carousel and plan to marry in a few months' time. Jack Ruby drives past and Olsen honks his horn to attract his attention. Ruby pulls over and opens his door. Olsen winds down his window and they start to talk.

He praises Ruby for closing the club out of respect for the president. Ruby rages against Oswald.

'Son of a bitch. It's too bad that a peon could do something like that.'

'If he was in England, they would drag him through the streets and would have hung him,' Kathy says.

Harry thinks that Oswald should be cut into ribbons inch by inch.

Ruby says how sorry he feels for Jackie and the children.

For the next hour Ruby, Olsen, Kay and Johnny Johnson the car park attendant talk about the assassination and how they despise Oswald. Kathy notices that Ruby has a stary, wild-eyed look, sometimes goes silent and stares into space.

In the White House, final preparations are being made in the East Room to receive the president's casket. A crucifix is brought in for Sargent Shriver to approve, but he thinks the wounds painted on Christ's body are too bloody, and asks for a simple, black crucifix from his bedroom to be used instead. Someone asks him if the casket will be open or closed.

'Jack didn't like to be touched. I doubt whether he'd like to be stared at now,' Shriver replies.

In Bethesda Hospital morgue, Joseph Hagan has finished dressing the body. Dave Powers chose a blue-grey suit from the eight that valet George Thomas brought from the White House, and a blue tie with light dots and black shoes. Thomas puts a handkerchief in the top suit pocket and hides its embroidered 'JFK', just as the president used to do. Hagan smoothes creases in the suit and puts the tie under a clasp. He puts a rosary in the president's hands, and the lid is closed.

2.56am/3.56am EST

In the corridor outside the morgue, an undertaker hands Lieutenant Bird an American flag, folded in a triangle. Gawler's have a large stock of these 5 ½ by 9 feet standard Veterans Administration issue flags, as they do so many military funerals.

The casket team stand either side of their dead commander in chief and pass the flag up the line, unfolding it as they do so. The flag, now fully unfurled, is stretched tight and dropped slowly over the casket.

3.05am/4.05am EST

Secret Service agents are loading the casket into the back of the Navy ambulance, which has been padded with blankets by Lieutenant Bird to prevent any damage (the ambulance is not designed to be a hearse). Jackie takes her place once again on one side of the casket and Robert Kennedy on the other, and then they draw the curtains.

Roy Kellerman tells the motorcycle police escort that he wants no sirens and a maximum speed of 30mph. Bill Greer is driving.

As the ambulance moves off for its ten-mile journey to the White House, naval personnel and their sleepy-looking children salute.

3.20am/4.20am EST

As the ambulance approaches Washington, scores of cars driven by members of the public are making an impromptu motorcade.

3.24am/4.24am EST

The president's body arrives at the White House. For parties, Jackie liked the entrance drive to be illuminated by flaming torches. Sargent Shriver has arranged for the torches to be lit once more.

Bill Greer drives his Boss a final few yards, and pulls up ahead of the honour guard of Marines.

As the military pall-bearers carry it up the steps of the portico, the casket tips up. Lieutenant Sam Bird, the officer in charge, grabs it and hears a Marine whisper, 'Good God, don't let go!'

The nine men carry the casket into the East Room and place it on the replica of President Lincoln's catafalque. General Godfrey McHugh stands next to Clint Hill and the room is so quiet they can hear each other breathe. Jackie arrives on the arm of Robert Kennedy, her clothing still covered in blood. Father John Kuhn reads the De Profundis, Psalm 130:

'Out of the depths I cry to you, O Lord; Lord hear my voice!

'My soul waits for the Lord more than sentinels wait for the dawn.'

Jackie walks up to the second floor, where she's met by her personal assistant Providencia Paredes. 'Provi' is shocked by the amount of blood on Mrs Kennedy's clothes. While she bathes, Provi packs them away in a bag, and hides it.

In the East Room, Robert Kennedy looks at his brother's body for the first time. Gawler's Funeral Home have done their best to disguise the injuries, but he decides that the body looks too much like a gruesome waxwork to be shown to the public. He asks for the casket to be closed.

At each corner of the casket is a flickering candle, and a soldier, his rifle at parade rest. The soldiers are known as the Deathwatch.

At the White House, Admiral Burkley is talking to Walter Jenkins, Lyndon Johnson's right-hand man. The doctor tells him that he has decided to retire.

4.00am/5.00am EST/10.00am GMT

The order for the Mannlicher-Carcano rifle is found by FBI

agents in the files of Klein's Sporting Goods in Chicago. It bears the name 'A Hidell, PO Box 2915, Dallas, Tex.' and was paid for by A Hidell – the name found in Oswald's wallet.

In the Lincoln bedroom, Robert Kennedy's old friend Charles Spalding is finding him a sleeping pill.

'God, it's so awful. Everything was beginning to run so well...' Robert says.

As Spalding closes the door he hears him break down and sob.

'Why, God?'

Outside the American embassy in London, a red-eyed American girl is talking to a reporter.

'I'm here because this is where you feel closest to your own country...'

Inside, hundreds of people are queuing to write in the book of condolence.

'With the death of President Kennedy every man in the Free World is a Kennedy.'

'God be with you.'

'Thank you, John Kennedy, for what your vitality gave the world.'

In Italy, the news that the president of the United States was killed by an Italian rifle is greeted with dismay. It becomes known as *'il fucile maledetto'* – 'that accursed gun'.

Jackie Kennedy is being given an injection of a half-gram of Amytal by her doctor John Walsh. An initial sedative didn't work, but within a few minutes, this second shot sends Jackie to sleep – for the first time since Suite 850 at the Hotel Texas.

4.45am/5.45am EST

Oswald's rifle is being carried across the White House lawn. Vince Drain has just landed by helicopter from Andrews Air Force Base, and is on his way to the Justice Department with his vital evidence, and for a meeting with J Edgar Hoover.

5.00am/6.00am EST/11.00am GMT

In London, Westminster Abbey's tenor bell has started tolling every minute. It will continue until noon – a tribute usually reserved only for dead monarchs.

Jack Ruby's strange nocturnal journey continues. He's now standing with his lodger George Senator and Carousel employee Larry Crafard in front of a billboard by the North Central expressway which says 'Impeach Earl Warren' (Warren is a US Supreme Court chief justice and considered too liberal by many Dallasites).

Ruby asks Crafard to take three Polaroids of the billboard. He then jots down a post office box number at the bottom of the billboard: '1754'. Ruby's convinced it's linked in some way to the black-bordered ad in the *Morning News*, which had a similar box number.

5.10am/6.10am EST

Clint Hill has arrived at his apartment in Arlington and is having something to eat with his wife Gwen, who's stayed up to see him. He will shortly shave, shower and head straight back to the White House. With the Johnson family to protect and funeral venues to search, all White House agents are having to work double shifts.

5.30am

At a downtown post office, Jack Ruby is talking through a grille to the night clerk. He wants to know who post office box 1754 belongs to. To his dismay it's full, indicating that the 'Impeach Earl Warren' billboard has had a good response.

'I can't give you any information. There is only one man can give it to you, and that is the postmaster of Dallas,' the clerk says.

6.00am

Apart from a waitress and a cashier, Ruby and George Senator are alone in the coffee shop of the Southland Hotel. Ruby's mood isn't improved by seeing yesterday's *Morning News* on the counter. He flicks through it and reads Weissman's black-bordered ad again. Ruby is furious that a fellow Jew should insult the president like that.

Senator has seen his landlord angry, but never as disturbed as this. His voice has a strange tone and his eyes have a blank stare.

6.30am/7.30am EST

On the third floor of the White House, Kenny O'Donnell is drinking and reminiscing about the late president with press secretary Pierre Salinger and valet George Thomas.

Once, when dressing in his bedroom for a flight on a stormy evening, the president had laughed and said to Thomas and presidential advisor Ted Sorenson, 'If that plane goes down, Lyndon will have this place cleared out from stem to stern in 24 hours – and you and George will be the first to go...'

Caroline Kennedy walks into her father's bedroom, half asleep. 'He's dead, isn't he?' she says to her grandmother.

Mrs Auchincloss can only nod.

7.30am/8.30am EST

In the early-morning gloom, John Metzler, the superintendent of the nation's largest military cemetery, is driving round Arlington's ten miles of roads looking for a suitable plot for the late president. He's had no phone call yet from the White House, but he knows that a funeral here is a possibility. Metzler is dismayed at the foot-high piles of autumn leaves, which won't look good on television.

7.40am/8.40am EST

Joe Kennedy still doesn't know of his son's death, although he suspects something is wrong. The family had decided that the 74-year-old, frail after a stroke two years before, needs to be shielded from the news.

But Joe, unable to speak, is becoming increasingly distressed. Ted and his sister Eunice are sitting by their father's bed.

'There's been a bad accident... The president has been hurt very badly.'

Joe Kennedy stares hard at his son.

'As a matter of fact, he died,' Ted says.

Joe Kennedy weeps for Jack and there is little Ted or Eunice can do to console him.

7.45am

In the barbershop of the Statler-Hilton, two barbers are discussing the assassination. One is convinced Lee Harvey

Oswald is guilty and should be executed; the other thinks that he deserves a fair trial. They have one customer who is keeping very quiet – Robert Oswald.

7.55am/8.55am EST

JFK's secretary Evelyn Lincoln is sitting in the Oval Office opposite the new president. She's wearing a pink suit, not appropriate for a day of mourning, but was in such a daze when she woke, she wasn't thinking straight.

'I have an appointment at 9.30am. Can I have my girls in your office by 9.30am?' Johnson says.

'I don't know, Mr President...' she replies, stunned that she only has half an hour to pack her things and leave.

8.00am/9.00am EST

The phone is ringing in press secretary Pierre Salinger's White House office; he's asleep in a chair. He answers, and hears a woman say, 'Mr Salinger, the president is calling.'

He smiles with relief – the shooting had clearly all been a terrible dream. Then he hears Lyndon Johnson's Texas drawl, and he's overcome with grief once more.

Robert Kennedy is in Evelyn Lincoln's office.

'Do you know he asked me to be out by 9.30?' she sobs. Kennedy's appalled and tracks down Johnson in the hall. Kennedy explains that packing up his brother's things will take time.

'Can you wait until noon?'

Johnson says that it's his advisors who are telling him that a speedy transition is necessary – but he can tell that Kennedy is unimpressed.

It is an unfortunate mix-up. On Johnson's desk in the Executive Office Building is a note from his secretary that he hasn't yet seen, telling him that she was mistaken, and that the late president's belongings will need another day to be cleared. Johnson won't return to the Oval Office for three days.

After five hours' sleep, Oswald is being woken up for a breakfast of stewed apricots, oatmeal, bread and coffee.

8.15am

Robert Oswald is tipping the barber who wanted his brother to have a fair trial 50 cents. Across town, Lee is being shaved by one of the jailers, as they won't let him have a razor.

8.20am/9.20am EST

At Arlington National Cemetery, Secretary of State for Defense Robert McNamara is standing in the rain. He knows that Kenny O'Donnell and the rest of the Irish Mafia want JFK buried in Boston at the family burial site, but McNamara agrees with Jackie that he should be buried on federal property, as he 'belongs to the people'. With him getting wet are the superintendent of the cemetery John Metzler, secretary of the Army Cyrus Vance, General Maxwell Taylor and Colonel Paul Miller. After his dawn drive, Metzler has identified three possible plots, and both he and McNamara like the slope below Arlington House best of all.

'Of course, it is now standard procedure for everyone buried here to have a grave of the same size,' Metzler says.

'What is the size?' McNamara asks.

'Six feet by ten.'

'Then the rules should be changed in this case. An

exception should be made for the president of the United States,' McNamara replies tersely.

8.40am

A journalist spots Robert Oswald standing outside Henry Wade's office.

'Your name is Robert Oswald, isn't it?'

'That's right.'

'You're 29 years old?'

'One question leads to another. Let's stop right there,' Oswald replies.

8.55am/9.55am EST

In the Family Dining Room, the first Catholic Mass in the history of the White House is about to be held for the Kennedy family and their close friends. The table has been taken out, chairs put in, and a makeshift altar set up. Jackie is walking in, a child on each hand. She abruptly stops.

'Oh no, I want it in the East Room where Jack is,' she says quietly.

Robert Kennedy asks Father John Cavanaugh to move the altar to the East Room. (Father Cavanaugh has only just recovered from being told bluntly by Jackie a few minutes before that for him to ask to hear her confession at a time like this was highly inappropriate.)

9.00am/3.00pm GMT

At all British football league matches, a minute's silence has begun. The flags on the stands are at half-mast and all the players are wearing black armbands.

In British newspapers the deaths of two influential writers, Aldous Huxley and CS Lewis, who died on the same day as President Kennedy, get only a brief mention.

Robert Oswald is talking with District Attorney Henry Wade. Wade's telling him about the overwhelming evidence he has that his brother shot Officer Tippit. Wade asks Robert about when he last saw Lee. He says not for almost a year. After some small talk he repeats the question. Robert smiles at this clumsy attempt to catch him out and check the truth of his story, and Wade laughs too.

Robert asks for passes to see his brother for himself, Marina and his mother. Wade phones Captain Fritz who says it's all been sorted for them to see Lee at noon.

Thomas B Thompson of *Life* magazine arrives at the Paines' house to take Marguerite, Marina and the children to the Adolphus Hotel, so they can be closer to City Hall and he can keep an eye on his exclusive. A *Life* photographer takes pictures as they pack, much to Marguerite's irritation.

9.10am/10.10am EST

For the Mass in the East Room, only a few people have seats, most are standing. Some are remembering that only 72 hours before they'd been in this very room for a smart reception, and had been dancing where the casket now rests. Outside it's still pouring with rain and the room is dark, illuminated by the dimmed chandeliers and by the four candles around the bier.

'Daddy's too big for that. How is he lying? Are his knees under his chin?' As she looks at the casket Caroline Kennedy is full of questions for Maud Shaw. The nanny tells her that it's bigger than it looks.

'Why can't I see him?'

'Only grown-ups can see him,' Maud replies.

> **Wesley Liebeler: Mr. Zapruder, I want to thank you very much, on behalf of the Commission, for coming down. It has been very helpful.**
>
> **Zapruder: Well, I am ashamed of myself. I didn't know I was going to break down... but it was a tragic thing, and when you started asking me that, and I saw the thing all over again... it was an awful thing and I loved the President, and to see that happen before my eyes – his head just opened up and shot down like a dog...**
>
> **Abraham Zapruder testimony for the Warren Commission**
> **22nd July 1964**

9.55am

In a small dark room in his dress factory next to the Book Depository, Abraham Zapruder is threading an 8mm film onto a projector. With him are Secret Service agents and the Los Angeles bureau chief of *Life* magazine, Richard B Stolley. The evening before, Stolley had been the first member of the national press to contact Zapruder, and he's here to see if the footage is worth buying.

The atmosphere in the room is tense. The projector whirrs into life and suddenly on the screen, in colour, is a brief shot of a small boy digging by a tree, then shots of three smiling people waiting for the motorcade, one of them waving at the camera. Then the president's limousine comes briefly into view, before disappearing behind a road sign. When it emerges, the president has his hands to his throat. Jackie turns to him. His head explodes as another bullet hits. There is no sound in the room, only the projector's motor. They see Clint Hill jump on the rear of the car and the camera shake as it accelerates into the darkness of the underpass and out of view. They have just witnessed the Secret Service lose its first president to an assassin. Stolley can sense the feeling of powerlessness from the agents around him.

10.00am/11.00am EST

Jackie Kennedy is standing in the Oval Office with Chief Usher JB West. After the Mass she'd asked him to walk over with her to the West Wing. Over the last two years they've worked closely together coordinating the redecoration of the White House, much needed after the more conservative Dwight and Mamie Eisenhower years. JB and Jackie get on well – he once helped her deter an unwanted house guest by pretending the Lincoln bedroom was being painted, by filling it with ladders, paint pots, dirty brushes and ashtrays filled with cigarette butts. When JFK gave the visitor a tour of the house he deliberately walked past the open Lincoln bedroom door, saying '...and of course this is where you would have spent the night, if Jackie hadn't been redecorating again.' When the president saw the ashtrays, Jackie told JB later, he almost cracked up laughing.

Now the two of them are watching the staff packing up her husband's things: family photographs, model ships, the rocking chair that he brought to the Oval Office to ease his back pain; the coconut shell from his PT-109 shipwreck, with its inscription that had saved him and his crew: '11 ALIVE NEED SMALL BOAT KENNEDY.'

Evelyn Lincoln is standing in the middle of the office, looking bewildered.

'I think we're probably in the way,' Jackie whispers to JB, and they leave.

The television in Joe Kennedy's room has been fixed, and he's lying in bed, propped up on pillows, watching pictures of the coffin in the East Room. Around him are copies of the *Boston Globe* and the *Boston Record American,* both with vivid accounts of his son's violent death.

10.10am

Chief Curry is taking questions from reporters who are still camped out on the third floor of City Hall. One is resting his book on Curry's back as he takes notes.

'With this man's apparent subversive background, was there any surveillance? Were police aware of his presence in Dallas?' Curry knows of Lieutenant Revill's account of his conversation with James Hosty.

'We in the Police Department here did not know he was in Dallas,' he says.

'Is it normally the practice of the FBI to inform the police?'

'Yes.'

'But you were not informed?'

'We had not been informed of this man.'

For the last few minutes, Abraham Zapruder has been running the seven seconds of film again and again as the room has filled up with journalists from other magazines and news agencies. He turns the lights on, and looks ill and exhausted.

To Richard Stolley, Zapruder seems almost apologetic that he, a humble dressmaker, is the one to have captured the moment of the murder. Stolley asks him for a word in private. As they walk into Zapruder's office, an Associated Press reporter shouts out, 'Don't make up your mind! Promise me you'll talk to us first. Promise!'

Waiting in the office is Zapruder's secretary Lillian Rogers. Stolley soon discovers that she was brought up not far from where he was in Illinois. Zapruder watches them talk, working out if Stolley can be trusted.

10.20am/11.20am EST

J Edgar Hoover calls the Dallas FBI office and orders the agent in charge, Gordon Shanklin, to get Chief Curry to retract his statement that the FBI knew about Oswald. Curry, who has a signed photo of Hoover on his office wall, does what he's told.

Robert Kennedy is at Arlington Cemetery. Originally favouring Boston, he too now likes the slope below Arlington House, even more so when it's pointed out that the proposed plot lines up perfectly with the White House and the Lincoln Memorial.

10.25am

Dallas Police Department deputy chief, MW Stevenson, is shouting instructions to the newsmen who are still crowding the third-floor corridor at City Hall.

'Whenever this [elevator] door is open and they come through here, we don't want any of you pushing him. We want to cooperate with you.'

'Do you mind if we shout a question at him?'

'I don't want you shouting a question at him in no way! The more you upset him the more difficult it is for us to talk to him.'

10.30am

Outside Abraham Zapruder's office, the journalists are getting frantic, resorting to passing their business cards under the door. Zapruder is desperately concerned that his film will end up being leered over in sleazy Time Square movie theatres. Stolley can tell that the dressmaker wishes he'd left the camera at home that morning, but that he also realises his 8mm film could make his family financially secure for life. Stolley keeps having to drive the price up.

> **At one time I told him, I said, 'You know you have killed the president, and this is a very serious charge.' He denied it and said he hadn't killed the president. He said people will forget that, and within a few days there would be another president.**
>
> **Captain Will Fritz testimony to the Warren Commission**
> **15th April 1964**

10.45am

Lee Harvey Oswald is being questioned once again by Captain Fritz. Fritz's job is being made harder by the fact that throughout his interrogations a stream of people are coming in and out of the room – members of the FBI, Secret Service, Postal Service and the district attorney's office.

Fritz tells Oswald that he knows he took a package to work with him the day of the assassination, and that he placed it in the back seat of Wesley Frazier's car, telling him they were curtain rods. Oswald denies it.

'Did you go toward the building carrying a long package?' Fritz says.

'No. I didn't carry anything but my lunch.'

Fritz then asks him about his bus and taxi rides and what he did when he got home. He's asked Oswald this before but is keen to trip him up.

'I changed my shirt and trousers and went to the movies.'

Fritz notices that he's changed his story. Yesterday he said he changed only his trousers.

Oswald asks for John Abt, a New York lawyer, to represent him. Fritz says that Oswald can use the prison phone and explains how he can get Abt's number. Assistant District Attorney Bill Alexander recognises Abt's name – he's a lawyer prominent in left-wing causes.

'This son of a bitch really is a communist,' he thinks.

10.50am

Robert Oswald walks into Suite 906 at the Adolphus Hotel to find it full of reporters and photographers from *Life* magazine. When he eventually finds his mother in the next room, he's not surprised to see her arguing with an FBI man called Brad Odum who wants to talk to Marina. She doesn't want Marina to talk to anyone. When Robert asks Marina if she'll talk to Odum, she says 'no'.

Richard Stolley is typing out a basic contract on Lillian Rogers' typewriter. Zapruder has agreed a $50,000 fee for print rights only. Stolley knows that it is worth much more, but Zapruder trusts Stolley and is happy that *Life* magazine will have his pictures. He signs, Stolley picks up the original film and a copy, and heads for the back door. He doesn't want to be around when his rivals find out that they've been beaten.

11.00am/12.00pm EST/5.00pm GMT

Alistair Cooke is in the BBC's New York radio studio at

Rockefeller Plaza, reading the final paragraph of his 794th 'Letter from America'. Three thousand miles away in the heart of Broadcasting House in London, a reel-to-reel tape recorder is capturing his words.

'...this charming, complicated, subtle, and gently intelligent man, whom the Western world was proud to call its leader, appeared for a split second in the telescopic sight of a maniac's rifle. And he was snuffed out. In that moment, all the decent grief of a nation was taunted and outraged. So that along with the sorrow, there is a desperate and howling note over the land. We may pray on our knees, but when we get up from them, we cry with the poet: 'Do not go gentle into that good night. Rage, rage against the dying of the light. Good night.'

There's a pause, and in New York the red light in the studio goes out. In London the tape machine stops recording.

11.10am/12.10pm EST

At the request of Jackie Kennedy, two Catholic priests, Monsignor Robert Paul Mohan and Father Gilbert Hartke, are beginning a vigil over her husband's casket. They will remain with it until the funeral.

Fritz asks Oswald where he was when Kennedy was shot. Oswald says he was having lunch with someone called Junior and another black employee, although he can't remember his name.

Fritz asks what belongings he keeps at the Paines' home. Oswald says sea bags, suitcases, kitchen items and clothes.

'What about a rifle?' Fritz asks.

Oswald denies again ever owning a rifle. Fritz asks Oswald if he belongs to the Communist Party. Oswald says he never joined and never had a card, but that he does belong to Fair

Play for Cuba and that he supports the Castro revolution.

Fritz asks him what he thinks of President Kennedy.

'I don't have anything to say about the president. He has a nice family, I admire his family.'

'You know you've killed the president, and this is a very serious charge.'

'I didn't kill him. People will forget his death in a few days and there will be another president.'

Fritz produces one of the Selective Service cards (a card that has information on those eligible for conscription) found in Oswald's wallet at the Texas Theater. It has a picture of Oswald, but the signature of Alex James Hidell.

'Did you sign this card Alex James Hidell?'

Oswald refuses to answer.

'This is your card?'

'I carried it, yes.'

'What did you use it for?'

Oswald refuses to comment. Harry Holmes, one of the interrogation team, reckons Oswald is almost enjoying himself.

11.27am

The interrogation over, Oswald is led though the waiting press. A microphone is waved in his face.

'I would like to contact Mr Abt, A-B-T. Mr Abt in New York to defend me,' Oswald says, and then he's led to his cell.

11.45am

NBC director Frederic Rheinstein is sitting in his remote TV truck, parked on the street in front of City Hall. The windows are open, but the curtains are drawn to keep sunlight off the monitors that are relaying pictures from the third floor. Suddenly light streams in as a curtain is pulled aside and a man puts his head inside the truck. Rheinstein ignores him – members of the public are doing this all the time. Jack Ruby watches for a while, pops his head back out and helps himself to one of the 14 fried chicken dinners that had been ordered for the TV crew.

In her second-floor office, Jackie Kennedy is keeping herself busy, making lengthy lists on White House stationery about what she has to do before the funeral on Monday. But she's also thinking of another's grief. One page is headed 'DALLAS POLICEMAN' and underneath 'Mrs Marie Tippitt (sic) Three children, 238 Glencairn Street Oak Cliff Texas – suburb of Dallas.'

'Brother, you won't find anything there.'

12.15pm

Texas law requires that a suspect, once charged, must be jailed in the county where the crime occurred. The press knows that their best chance to see Oswald is when he's transferred 11 blocks to the county jail in Dealey Plaza and into the care of Sheriff Bill Decker.

'Chief Curry, what are your plans now in dealing with Oswald himself? Will he be interrogated here further or will he be transferred to the county jail to await presentment to the grand jury?' a journalist asks.

'He will go to the county jail. I don't know just when,' Curry replies.

1.07pm

'Mr Wade, how soon can we expect a trial?' asks a reporter.

'I'd say around the middle of January' says the district attorney, leaning on the third-floor corridor wall.

'And will you conduct the trial?'

'Yes, sir. I plan to.'

'And will you ask for the capital verdict?'

'We'll ask for the death penalty.'

'In how many cases of this type have you been involved, that is, when the death penalty is involved?'

'Since I've been district attorney we've asked... I've asked the penalty in 24 cases.'

'How many times have you obtained it?'

'Twenty-three.'

1.15pm/ 2.15pm EST

John Metzler, the superintendent at Arlington, is driving a tent peg into the waterlogged earth, watched by Jackie Kennedy, sheltering under an umbrella. Moments before, with a nod, she'd agreed that this should be the plot for her husband's grave.

1.30pm/2.30pm EST

President Johnson has called a Cabinet meeting at the White House. As they walk into the Cabinet Room, they can see JFK's rocking chair upside down in a packing case. Robert Kennedy arrives late, just as Johnson is in the middle of reading a prepared statement. For many in the Cabinet it's the first time they've seen the attorney general since his brother's murder, and they are shocked at how grief-stricken he looks.

Johnson is furious. He thinks Kennedy's late arrival is a deliberate snub.

Passes to see Lee arrive for Marguerite and Marina, but there isn't one for Robert. Marguerite offers hers but he insists she takes it.

1.35pm

Robert Oswald is being interviewed by Secret Service agent Mike Howard and he's telling him about the volatile relationship between his mother and brother.

'These personal details will be of special interest to Mrs Kennedy,' Howard says.

'I would like to take this opportunity to express to Mrs Kennedy, through you...' Oswald begins, but his voice breaks.

'That's all right, I know what you're trying to say,' Howard replies.

1.40pm

The Police Department jail visiting room is divided by a grubby panel of thick glass, and on each side are eight cubicles containing a shelf and a phone, but no chairs.

Lee and Marina Oswald are using the telephones. Inside her shoe Marina has hidden the photos of her husband with the rifle. Marguerite hangs back, watching.

'Why did you bring that fool with you? I don't want to talk to her,' he says pointing to Marguerite.

'She's your mother. Of course she came. Have they been beating you in prison?'

'Oh, no, they treat me fine. You're not to worry about that. Did you bring June and Rachel?'

'They're downstairs. Can we talk about anything we like?'

'Of course, we can speak about *absolutely* anything at all.'

Marina takes his sarcastic tone to be a warning to say nothing.

'They asked me about the gun.'

'Oh, that's nothing and you're not to worry if there's a trial. It's a mistake, I'm not guilty.'

But Marina can see that he's afraid, and she starts to cry. His eyes fill too.

Marguerite, who hadn't understood their conversation, as it was in Russian, is given the phone by Marina.

'Honey, you are so bruised up, your face. What are they doing?'

'Mother, don't worry, I got that in a scuffle.'

'Is there anything I can do to help you?'

'No, Mother, everything is fine. I know my rights.'

Marina takes the phone again.

Lee tells her, 'You're not to worry. You have friends. They'll help you. If it comes to that, you can ask the Red Cross for help. Kiss Junie and Rachel for me.'

'Remember I love you.'

As Lee is led away by a guard, he keeps looking at Marina the whole time.

Marina knows he's guilty; she saw it in his eyes. He seemed different – as if pleased that after General Walker, he had at last succeeded.

It is the last time she sees her husband alive.

1.55pm

Oswald is calling John Abt's office in New York, but there's no reply. He'd tried his home number first, but with no luck.

Abt is spending the weekend with his wife in a cabin in Connecticut that has no television or radio. (When reporters finally track him down in a few hours' time, he says that he can't defend Oswald because of his legal commitments.)

2.00pm/3.00pm EST

Dallas Police detective Guy Rose, accompanied by four colleagues, is making a thorough search of the Paines' garage. They've been sifting through the Oswalds' belongings for almost an hour.

'Look at this!' Rose suddenly shouts, holding up two negatives and a snapshot of Oswald holding the rifle. Rummaging in the same box, they find a page torn from the February issue of *American Rifleman,* advertising guns available from Klein's Sporting Goods in Chicago. A Mannlicher-Carcano rifle is circled in pen. The rifle, it says, shows 'only slight use' and is 'ready for shooting'.

(In the weeks after the assassination, Klein's would receive orders from 150 people in Dallas for a Mannlicher-Carcano rifle.)

In a light aircraft in the sky above Dealey Plaza, George Phenix of CBS News is filming a queue of cars driving slowly past the spot where Kennedy was killed; it's a mile long.

Jackie Kennedy wants the funeral service to be held in Washington at the Cathedral of St Matthew the Apostle, eight blocks away from the White House. The Catholic Church prefers the Shrine of the Immaculate Conception – it's grander and larger. Robert Kennedy agrees that St Matthew's is the wrong place.

'I think it's too small. It only seats eleven hundred.'

'I don't care. They can all stand in the streets. I just know it's the right place to have it,' Jackie replies.

But there's another reason. She wants to walk behind her husband's coffin, not ride in a 'fat black Cadillac', and the Shrine of the Immaculate Conception is too far away to go on foot.

Researchers at the Library of Congress are then given the

task of seeing if there is a precedent for such a march.

Joe Kennedy is a formidable father and businessman. After the death of his eldest son, Joe Jr, in the Second World War, he'd pushed Jack into politics.

In 1957 JFK told a reporter, 'It was like being drafted. My father wanted his eldest son in politics. "Wanted" isn't the right word. He demanded it.'

Even at his age, Joe is still a force to be reckoned with. After lunch, Ann Gargan, his niece and full-time nurse, found him struggling to get dressed. He made it clear that he wanted to get to Washington, and nothing she could say would dissuade him. Ann drove him to Boston airport, but the only plane he's prepared to fly in, JFK's private plane *Caroline*, wasn't there, so now she and Joe are sitting in the car, watching the jets take off and land.

2.15pm

The two cab drivers involved in Friday's drama, William Whaley, who picked Oswald up in downtown Dallas, and William Scoggins, who witnessed the shooting of Officer Tippit, are sitting waiting in the dark line-up room to identify the suspect. Even before he sees him, Whaley recognises his passenger, just by his voice. Oswald is shouting at the police, telling them it isn't right to put him in a line-up with a bunch of teenagers younger than him.

'I know what you're doing! You're trying to railroad me! I want my lawyer!'

Scoggins recognises Oswald straight away.

'Well, he can bitch and holler all he wants, but that's the man I saw running from the scene. Number 3.' Scoggins holds up three fingers to the detective next to him.

2.30pm

Jack Ruby likes to use Nichol's Garage, round the corner from the Carousel, as an extension of his office. He's on the garage manager's phone calling the newsroom of radio station KLIF.

'Who is this?' Ruby asks.

'This is Ken Dowe.'

'Is there a newsman or somebody I can talk to? This is Jack Ruby.'

Dowe is a presenter who's helping out on a very busy news day. He's only been in Dallas a month, but already knows Ruby as someone who sorts girls for record pluggers when they're visiting Dallas.

'I understand they are moving Oswald over to the county jail. Would you like for me to go over there and get some news stories? Would you like me to cover it, because I am a pretty good friend of Henry Wade's, and I believe I can get some stories,' Ruby says.

'Mr Ruby, if you want to help us any way you can, we will appreciate it,' replies Dowe.

Ruby puts the phone down.

'I'm acting like a reporter!' he says to the garage attendant.

3.15pm

A cameraman is filming Robert Oswald who is standing alone in the jail visiting room, waiting to see his brother. To Oswald's irritation, he's been filming for a while, the whirr of the camera filling the silence. He's amazed at the freedom the police have given the press in City Hall.

Suddenly he sees his brother casually strolling towards his cubicle. Lee picks up the phone on his side and says when

Robert picks up his, 'This is taped.'

He can see that Lee has a cut over his right eye and a bruised cheek. 'What have they been doing to you? Were they roughing you up?'

'I got this at the theatre. They haven't bothered me since. They're treating me all right.'

Robert is amazed at how calm and matter-of-fact he is. After some small talk, Robert can't hold back any longer.

'Lee, what the Sam Hill is going on?'

'I don't know.'

'You don't know?! Look, they've got your pistol, they've got your rifle, they've got you charged with shooting the president and a police officer. And you tell me you don't know!'

Lee straightens up and his expression changes.

'I just don't know what they are talking about. Don't believe this so-called evidence,' he says firmly.

Robert is looking closely at him as he speaks. He has just realised something chilling – his brother is unconcerned about his plight. Robert looks into his eyes, but they are blank.

'Brother, you won't find anything there,' Lee says softly.

After a silence they talk about Marina and the fact that June needs a new pair of shoes. Robert asks about John Abt, the attorney his brother has been trying to reach.

'I'll get you an attorney down here,' Robert says.

'No, you stay out of it!'

'Stay out of it? It looks like I've already been dragged into it!'

'Well, I'm not going to have anyone from down here.'

His brother's answers are mechanical, and not the Lee he knows.

A police officer comes into the room, taps Lee on the shoulder, and then waits for the brothers to finish their conversation.

'I'll see you in a day or two,' Robert says.

'Now you've got your job and everything, don't be running

back and forth all the time and getting in trouble with your boss.'

'Don't worry about that. I'll be back.'

'All right. I'll see you,' Lee says, and puts down the phone.

Those are the last words the brothers will ever say to each other. The cameraman keeps filming as Robert takes the elevator downstairs.

3.25pm

The public has heard rumours that Oswald is about to be moved to the county jail at Dealey Plaza. CBS reporter Dan Rather is broadcasting live from City Hall.

'All day long, crowds have built up and waned and then again built up, as people come by just to look at the spot, walk round the wreath... the crowd now has moved to the sidewalk facing the county jail. Not many people at this moment are looking at the building where the shot came; most of the people have seen it. Now they are waiting for a glimpse of Lee Harvey Oswald...'

Captain Fritz, Chief Curry and Jack Ruby are among those looking at the wreaths.

4.00pm

Abraham Zapruder's phone rings. He answers – it's yet another news agency who's heard that *Life* have bought only the print rights to his film, and asking if he'd sell the motion picture rights. Zapruder is tired, and tells them that he doesn't want to talk about it until Monday.

> *I can't give the specific words to this part but I carry a clear impression... that he sounded to me almost as if*

nothing out of the ordinary had happened. [Assuming] I would make this telephone call for him, would help him, as I had in other ways previously. He expressed gratitude to me. I felt, but did not express, considerable irritation at his seeming to be so apart from the situation, so presuming of his own innocence, if you will, but I did say I would make the call for him.

Ruth Paine testimony to the Warren Commission
20th March 1964

Ruth Paine's phone is ringing.

'This is Lee.'

'Well, hi!' Ruth says.

He asks her to call John Abt in New York and to ask him to be his attorney. Oswald gives her two numbers for Abt, and tells her to call him after 6pm when long-distance rates are cheaper. Ruth is extremely irritated at Oswald's manner – acting as if nothing has happened. But she agrees to make the call, then hangs up. The phone rings again – it's Lee, and he makes the same request almost word for word.

4.10pm

At Sol's Turf Bar on Commerce Street, Jack Ruby is arguing incoherently with his friend, jeweller Frank Bellocchio. Bellocchio is blaming Dallas for the assassination and says he plans to sell up and quit the city.

'The city was good enough for you before all this!' says Ruby.

Bellocchio shows him the black-bordered Weissman ad to prove his point, which winds Ruby up even more – claiming it's the work of a group trying to stir up anti-Jewish feeling.

Ruby then shows Bellocchio his Polaroids of the 'Impeach

Earl Warren' billboard, but refuses to give him one, saying it was his scoop, and he wanted to give them to 'the right person'. Bellocchio hasn't a clue what Ruby is talking about.

4.23pm/10.23pm GMT

At BBC Television Centre in London, the live satirical programme *That Was The Week That Was* has just started. They've scrapped the hour-long format and have written, from scratch, in a day, a 20-minute special, about Kennedy's death.

'The reason why the shock was so great, why when one heard the news last night one felt suddenly so empty,' says host David Frost, 'was because it was the most unexpected news one could possibly imagine... We didn't believe in assassination any more, not in the "civilised" world anyway...'

Dame Sybil Thorndike reads a poem, '...yesterday the sun was shot out of your sky, Jackie...'; the show's regular singer, Millicent Martin, standing against a backdrop of a sunset, sings a song written that afternoon by Herbert Kretzmer, called 'In the Summer of His Years'. As she finishes the performance, a tear rolls down her cheek.

The programme will be shown 24 hours later on NBC, and a year later, an LP of the programme will win a Grammy.

4.40pm

In Suite 906 of the Adolphus Hotel, the team from *Life* magazine are offering Robert Oswald sandwiches, as he hasn't eaten anything all day. They don't ask him about the meeting with his brother, and for that he's grateful. Marguerite and Marina are no longer there, having been moved by *Life* to the Executive Inn Motel near Love Field, to keep them away from other journalists who have found out where they are.

Chief Justice Earl Warren, watching events unfold on television, is horrified that the evidence against Oswald is being paraded for the cameras by Curry and District Attorney Wade. He knows that even if Oswald is found guilty by a Texas court, the Supreme Court could reverse the verdict, because of the way the case is being handled.

At least 24 Americans don't know that their President has died. The jurors on two murder trials – one in Mineola, Long Island, the other in Blountville, Tennessee, are cut off from the outside world. The two judges are concerned that news of the assassination in the middle of a murder trial might sway their judgement. Telephone calls are banned and taxi drivers and hotel staff are forbidden to mention it.

NBC director Frederic Rheinstein is still in his remote TV truck watching the camera feeds from the third floor. To his surprise, he sees the man who poked his head through the truck window that morning pass by their cameras and go into District Attorney Wade's office. No reporters are allowed in there, and Rheinstein can't work out how this man can just stroll in.

'That's the creep who was by the truck!' he says on talkback to the cameraman on the third floor.

'He's just told us that he knows Wade personally and can get him to come out and talk to us,' the floor manager replies.

An engineer in the truck joins in, saying how earlier he saw the man take one of their fried chicken dinners.

5.10pm

Jack Ruby is handing out Carousel cards to the reporters in City Hall and promising free drinks.

5.20pm/6.20 EST

Secretary of Defense McNamara is on his fourth visit of the day to Arlington; he's soaked and his shoes squelch when he walks. He's feeling cold, wet and miserable.

With a team from the Army Corps of Engineers, he's just marked out a perimeter for the grave site. Now he's walking down the slope with Paul Fugua, a college student who works part-time at Arlington House. The young man is telling him that when the president visited Arlington House on 3rd March, he'd overheard him say that it had the most beautiful view in Washington. More than ever, McNamara feels they are doing the right thing.

5.45pm

H Louis Nichols, the president of the Dallas Bar Association, is sitting opposite Oswald in his cell.

'Do you have a lawyer?'

'Well, I really don't know what this is all about, I've been incarcerated, and kept incommunicado. Do you know a lawyer called John Abt?'

Nichols doesn't.

'Either Mr Abt or someone who is a member of the American Civil Liberties Union, and if I can find a lawyer here who believes in anything I believe in, and believes as I believe, and believes in my innocence...' Oswald pauses, '...as much as he can, I might let him represent me.'

'What I am interested in knowing is right now, do you want me or the Dallas Bar Association to try to get you a lawyer?'

'No, not now. You might come back next week, and if I don't get some of these other people to represent me, I might ask you to get somebody to represent me.'

Researchers in the Library of Congress have discovered more than one precedent for Mrs Kennedy's request to walk to her husband's funeral Mass. Similar processions followed the bodies of George Washington, Abraham Lincoln, Ulysses S. Grant and Teddy Roosevelt through the streets of Washington. The funeral will take place at St Matthew's.

6.00pm

In a farmhouse in the small town of Boyd, Texas, Robert Oswald is discussing with his wife Vada and her parents the safest place for them to be. They are all convinced that someone might try and attack them, in revenge for the president's death.

After 6pm, as requested, Ruth Paine is calling the two numbers that Oswald gave her for John Abt, but with no success.

Bob Huffaker of KRLD News is talking to Chief Curry.

'Chief, none of us has slept more than a couple of hours since Friday. These guys need some rest. Can you just tell me how early we need to be set up, so that we don't miss the transfer?'

'If your men will be here by 10 o'clock in the morning, that will be early enough for you.'

Earlier, one of Curry's detectives, Jim Leavelle, had suggested that they 'double-cross' the media and move Oswald without warning, as it made no sense to move him in public and at a time that everyone knew. (Leavelle has also had a bellyful of the reporters on the third floor.)

'I've promised them they'd see the man moved. I want them to see we haven't abused him. And the only way to do that is to let them view the transfer,' Curry had replied. A public transfer is the advice from the Sam Bloom public relations agency, who Curry's bosses have employed.

6.30pm

The Dallas Police have made an 8x10 enlargement of the backyard photograph of Oswald with his rifle that they found in the Paines' garage. Fritz shows it to Oswald, who is thrown for a moment. He says that he won't say anything without an attorney being present.

'Is this your photograph?' Fritz asks.

'Well, that's just a fake. The face is mine but it's been superimposed on the body of someone else. I've been photographed by the news media numerous times as I go to line-ups or to Homicide, and that's probably how you got the photograph of my face. I know all about photography, I worked with photography for a long time. That is a picture that someone else has made. I never saw that picture in my life.'

'Wait just a minute, and I'll show you one you have seen probably,' Fritz says, and shows him the smaller, original photograph.

'I never have seen that picture, either. That is a picture that has been reduced from the big one.'

Outside in the corridor, Chief Curry is talking to the press. Amazingly, they already know in detail about the photographs. Curry says that even as they speak Captain Fritz is confronting Oswald with the pictures. He also tells them that the FBI has discovered the order for the rifle from Klein's in Chicago, and that it matches Oswald's handwriting.

6.45pm

J Edgar Hoover hears that once again Curry is giving out details of evidence passed to them by the FBI, and he's furious. He phones Gordon Shanklin, the FBI agent in charge, and tells him to go and see Curry and insist he doesn't go on air again until the case is over.

7.45pm

Ruby is raging to his sister about the 'Impeach Earl Warren' billboard and the Weissman advert, saying that he thinks it's a gentile using a false name to blame it all on the Jews. She listens, thinking that her brother is nuts.

He asks Eva, who is recovering from surgery, if she would be well enough to go with him to the Tippit funeral on Monday. He goes to the funerals of all Dallas police officers killed on duty – on one occasion he even took along all his strippers.

8.30pm

In her room at the Executive Inn Motel, Marina Oswald takes her copies of the photograph from her shoe, tears them in half, and sets light to them in an ashtray. They don't burn very well, so she flushes them down the toilet.

9.30pm

Ruth Paine's phone rings and when she answers she hears Lee say in Russian, 'Marina, please.'

It's the phrase he uses every time he wants to speak to his wife.

'She's not here. I've got an idea where she might be, but I'm not certain.'

'She should be at your house! Tell her that she should be at your house!' he says, irritated.

Ruth tells him that she'll try and pass on the message. She knows exactly where Marina is, and once Oswald has hung up, she calls the Executive Inn. Marguerite answers, and Ruth tells her that Lee had called, and that he wants Marina to stay at Ruth's home.

'Well, he is in prison. He don't know the things we are up against, the things we have to face. What he wants doesn't really matter.'

Ruth is shocked at her selfishness, and her lack of concern for her son's wishes.

One of Jack's strippers, who performs as 'Little Lynn', but whose real name is Karen Carlin, is sitting in the Colony Club next door to the Carousel, dialling her boss's home number. Karen and her husband Bruce have driven from Fort Worth to find out if the Carousel is going to open; they're broke and need money urgently. She's 19 and four months pregnant. Ruby is angry when he hears what she wants.

'Don't you have any respect for the president? Don't you know the president is dead?'

'Jack, I am sorry. Andrew [Armstrong, the Carousel's bartender] said that perhaps we would be open, and I don't have any money, and you know I am supposed to get paid. And I need some money to get back home.'

'I don't know when I will open. I don't know if I will ever open back up,' Ruby says.

10.00pm/11.00pm EST

Jackie Kennedy is writing her husband a letter.

10.10pm

Ruby's sister Eva is in her bedroom, looking at the bed where her brother had slept solidly for an hour earlier – something he'd never done before. She notices that his hair oil has left a stain on her new $20.50 bedspread. Eva vows to give him hell about it tomorrow.

10.30pm

Bruce Carlin is calling Jack Ruby from Nichol's Garage (he and Karen left the Colony Club as they had no money to pay for drinks). Ruby had promised to come down to the Carousel Club within the hour and pay his wife an advance on her salary, but he hasn't showed. Ruby asks to speak to garage attendant Huey Reeves, and persuades him to lend the Carlins $5 to get home. Karen signs a receipt for it and they drive back to Fort Worth.

11.00pm

Jack Ruby is paying Huey Reeves, the attendant at Nichol's Garage, the $5 he owes him.

00.10am Saturday 23rd November: Lee Harvey Oswald being led through the Dallas Police Department

Sunday 24th November 1963

In a gymnasium at Fort Myer, Washington, the eight pipers of the Scottish Black Watch Regiment are rehearsing for the president's funeral, playing the traditional British Army slow lament 'Flowers of the Forest'. Eleven days earlier, they'd performed on the White House lawn at an event for a thousand underprivileged children. JFK, Jackie, Caroline and John Jr watched from a balcony. Pipe Major JB Anderson then presented President Kennedy with a Black Watch dirk (a small dagger), engraved with the regimental motto 'Nobody wounds us with impunity'. 'I think that is a very good motto for some of the rest of us!' he'd joked.

The Black Watch pipers had then begun a tour of the States and were in Kentucky when they got the call that Mrs Kennedy wanted them to play at her husband's funeral. She'd remembered how he'd loved the bagpipes that day, and had spoken of his affection for Scotland.

Pipe Major JB Anderson is coming into the gym from a White House briefing with news that their rehearsal is to be abandoned for the night. He's discovered that the US military march at a faster pace at funerals than the British, and so new pieces of music will have to be rehearsed in the morning.

A couple of the Black Watch pipers look in a bad way, with bruises, cuts and stitches on their faces – they'd got into a brawl in Kentucky on the evening of the assassination. Both Catholics, they'd said in a bar how tragic it was that the president had been shot, and had been promptly set upon by anti-Kennedy Protestants.

00.45am

Jack Ruby is making his final call of the day, to his sister Eva, to see how she's feeling.

1.15am

Darwin Payne of the *Dallas Times Herald* dials the home number of Chief Curry. He wants to check a story he's heard, that there's an eyewitness who can identify Oswald as the killer. The newsdesk needs the story confirmed as soon as possible. Woken by the phone, Curry's wife puts her husband on, but Payne can't get any sense from him, and he reckons that the chief must have taken sleeping pills. After writing pages of notes, hoping something he says might make sense, Payne gives up. Curry's wife takes the phone off the hook.

2.30am

'I would like to speak to the man in charge.'

In the FBI office in Dallas, 20-year-old support clerk Vernon R Glossup is answering a call.

'The special agent in charge is not in at the present time. Is there someone else who can help you?' Glossup says.

'Just a minute.' There's a pause and Glossup thinks he can hear the phone being passed to someone else.

'I represent a committee that is neither right nor left wing and tonight, tomorrow morning, or tomorrow night we are going to kill the man that killed the president. There will be no excitement and we will kill him. We wanted to be sure to tell the FBI, Police Department, and Sheriff's Office. We will be there and we will kill him.'

The man hangs up.

Shortly after, Deputy Sheriff CC McCoy gets an identical call, except this time the voice says that 'a hundred of us will see that he is dead'.

5.15am

Captain William B Frazier of the Dallas Police is calling Captain Fritz at home, confident that as an early riser, he'll be awake. He tells him about the anonymous threat made to Oswald. Fritz says that the transfer is Chief Curry's responsibility, and that Frazier should call him instead. Fritz tries Curry's home number but can't get through.

> *During my first visit at their apartment... the second time I saw Marina, I suggested to [Oswald] that he should insist that she learn English as quickly as possible because it would be so much easier for her to get along in this country, and he replied that he would prefer that she did not learn English at all, or else he would lose his fluency in the Russian language. So it showed to me that he didn't particularly care about her. He cared more about himself...*
>
> **Peter Gregory testimony to the Warren Commission**
> **13th March 1964**

6.30am

Three weeks ago, Marguerite Oswald had started learning Russian at her local library, in the hope that if Lee and Marina got in touch (they hadn't spoken for a year), she could converse with her daughter-in-law. This morning Marguerite had woken up feeling alone and abandoned by *Life* magazine. Her grandchildren need diapers and there's no way they can go into Dallas to get some. Marguerite doesn't know how to get hold of Robert and she distrusts Ruth Paine. So she's decided to call her Russian language teacher, Peter Gregory. Gregory is still in bed.

'Mr Gregory, I need your help. The reporters, the news media are badgering me. I wonder if some of your friends or you could provide a place for me to hide from them.'

It sounds to Gregory as if she is crying, although he doesn't think that she's the crying type.

'I'm sorry, but I won't talk to anyone I don't know.'

'I would rather not tell you who I am, but I shall identify myself by saying I am one of the students in the Russian class in the library.'

Gregory in fact knows exactly who it is, and from where she's calling. The day before, Mike Howard of the Secret Service had asked him to come to the Executive Inn to translate for him when he interviewed Marina. In the end Gregory wasn't needed.

Gregory had already met Marina and Lee a few times, after Lee came to him the previous year looking for a job as a Russian translator. Marguerite doesn't know of this connection.

'Now, I'll tell you what I will do, Mrs Oswald, you stay where you are and I will promise to you that I will come to see you sometime today.'

He hangs up and calls Mike Howard, who says he'll find a secure place for Marguerite, Marina and the children.

A squad car has arrived outside Chief Curry's home and two officers are banging on his door, trying to wake him up.

8.45am

Mike Howard has called Robert Oswald, who is staying at his parents-in-law's farm, and is telling him that Marguerite had phoned complaining that she can't get any rest, because of the press disturbing her. They both agree that Marguerite and Marina should move out of the Executive Motel and stay at the farm.

9.00am

Over a breakfast of scrambled eggs and grapefruit juice, Jack Ruby's lodger is watching him with concern. George Senator thinks Ruby looks like he's in shock; he's mumbling so badly that Senator can't understand what he's saying. Their cleaning lady Elnora Pitts had called earlier and had been so disturbed by Ruby's voice that she'd decided not to come round.

'He don't sound right to me over the phone. I'm going to wait,' she told her daughter.

'This Keystone Kops situation...'

9.10am

Chief Curry is back at work in City Hall. He and Sheriff Decker have decided that the Police Department should transfer Oswald, rather than Decker's men, who would normally do the job, as they have more men available.

Curry is talking to Assistant Chief Charles Batchelor.

191

'What do you think about getting an armoured truck?'

'I think I know where I can get one,' Batchelor replies.

To drive into the basement of City Hall you go down an entrance ramp from Main Street, and you exit via a ramp up to Commerce Street. On one side of the ramp is a car park for City Hall employees and on the other, the jail office and elevator. A railing divides the car park from the ramp. Curry's plan is that Oswald will be taken down in the elevator and put into the back of the armoured truck (used by banks to move money) waiting on the ramp, and then escorted by two police cars to the county jail at Dealey Plaza.

In preparation, officers are clearing the basement car park and ramp of press, and guards are being posted on the exit and entrance ramps as well as the five doorways to the car park. When it's completed, the members of the press who have passes will be allowed back in.

9.30am

It's crowded in Captain Fritz's office. When Oswald comes in, he's facing seven men, keen to ask him questions.

'Are there any FBI in here?' he asks.

'No, no FBI men,' replies Captain Fritz.

'Well, who is that man?' he says pointing at Harry Holmes.

'He's a postal inspector [part of the law enforcement arm of the US Postal Service] and he has a few questions for you.'

This morning Holmes had been on his way to church, when he felt that he should really be at the Police Department continuing with the interrogation of Oswald.

'I'm going down to see if I can do something for Captain Fritz. I imagine he is as sleepy as I am,' Holmes had told his wife.

9.45am

Radio reporter Ike Pappas and Jerry O'Leary of the *Washington Star* are practising running down the stairs of City Hall. They want to be able to interview Oswald as he comes out of Fritz's office and then be able to beat the elevator to the basement, so they can see him getting in the armoured truck.

10.00am

'My Dear Caroline... you must have a lot of courageous blood in your veins. No one can erase this day... you will cry. (My children did, my wife did, and I did.) You will miss him. (We will.) You will be lonely for him... you will want to know why anyone would do a thing like this to your father. Most of all, God will help you...'

Jack Ruby is sitting in his apartment in his boxer shorts with tears in his eyes, reading a letter printed in the *Dallas Times Herald*. He then reads an article on the facing page that says that Mrs Kennedy may have to return to Dallas for Oswald's trial.

Robert Oswald is in a phone booth in Fort Worth getting directions from Secret Service agent Mike Howard. He's on his way to see his mother at the Executive Inn Motel in Dallas, but isn't sure how to get there. Howard says that they should meet up halfway, so he can take Robert there himself. They can also rendezvous with translator Peter Gregory.

10.10am

The interrogation of Oswald is on familiar territory.

'Do you own a rifle?" Fritz is asking.

'No.'

'Well, have you shot a rifle since you have been out of the Marines?'

'No. Well, possibly a small bore, maybe a .22, but not anything larger since I left the Marine Corps.'

'Do you own a rifle?'

'Absolutely not. How would I afford a rifle? I make $1.25 an hour. I can't hardly feed myself.'

'What about this picture of you holding this rifle?'

'I don't know what you are talking about…'

10.19am

Karen Carlin, who called the night before about getting paid, is again on the phone to Jack Ruby.

'I've called, Jack, to try to get some money, because the rent is due and I need some money for groceries, and you told me to call.'

'Can't you wait until payday?'

'Jack, you're going to be closed.'

'How much will you need?' Ruby replies.

'About $25.'

'Well, I have to go downtown anyway, so I will send it to you by Western Union. It will take a while as I have to get dressed. What name do I send it to?'

'Karen Bennett. I sure would appreciate it.'

She puts the phone down thinking how distracted he sounded.

Harry Holmes is asking Oswald about the various post office boxes he's used in the last year. Oswald tells Holmes nothing he doesn't know already. He thinks that Oswald is so disciplined and quick-witted, he'll never confess to Kennedy's murder.

10.30am

Marina is keen to see pictures of Lee on the hotel room television. But Marguerite has seen enough.

'Oh, honey, let's turn the television off. It's the same thing over and over.'

So they turn it off.

Dallas Times Herald photographer Bob Jackson is in the City Hall basement with about 30 other members of the press, and what he estimates to be about 70 cops. On Friday he was in the Kennedy motorcade, and when the shots were fired he looked up and saw the rifle sticking out of the sixth-floor Book Depository window, but his camera was out of film. His disappointment at missing an award-winning shot is exacerbated by the fact that two days on, loud noises make him a nervous wreck. A truck backfired as he drove in this morning and gave him a sudden flashback to Friday and Dealey Plaza.

Jackson has photographed plenty of prison transfers before. His plan today is to pre-focus on a spot about ten feet in front of him, get that shot and then run up the ramp to get shots of Oswald getting in the armoured truck. To his right is Frank Johnson from UPI, to his left, Jack Beers of the *Dallas Morning News*.

10.55am

Jack Ruby is crying as he drives his white 1960 Oldsmobile past the many wreaths in Dealey Plaza. He can see crowds outside the jail, so he reckons Oswald has already been moved.

At the Parkland Hospital, administrator Peter Geilich is asking the staff nurse in the Emergency Room to stop her team from going to lunch until the Oswald transfer is over. He saw the crowds outside the county jail on television and he fears that they might try and attack Oswald. Geilich then goes to see the switchboard operators and warns them there may be emergency calls.

> *….[the] thought never entered my mind prior to that Sunday morning when I took it upon myself to try to be a martyr or some screwball, you might say. But I felt very emotional and very carried away for Mrs Kennedy, that with all the strife she had gone through… I had been following it pretty well… that someone owed it to our beloved president that she shouldn't be expected to come back to face trial of this heinous crime.*
>
> **Jack Ruby testimony to the Warren Commission**
> **7th June 1964**

11.00am

'What religion are you?' Secret Service agent Kelley asks Oswald.

'I have no faith. I suppose you mean the Bible…'

'Yes.'

'Well, I have read the Bible. It is fair reading, but not very interesting. But, as a matter of fact, I am a student of philosophy and I don't consider the Bible as even a reasonable or intelligent philosophy. I don't think much of it,' Oswald says.

'Do you believe in a deity?' asks Fritz.

'I don't care to discuss that with you!' Oswald snaps back.

By now, Chief Curry is losing patience. The interrogation of Oswald is taking longer than he expected. He wanted him transferred an hour ago. Although the blinds in his office are down, Fritz can still make out Curry pacing up and down outside.

11.05am

Two armoured trucks have arrived. Assistant Chief Batchelor is peering inside the smaller one. He prefers the larger truck as it has space in the back for a prisoner and two guards.

11.10am

The larger armoured truck proved too tall to get under the eight-foot Main Street entrance ramp that leads down to the basement, so Assistant Chief Batchelor told the driver (who's just been pulled out of teaching Sunday School for this last-minute job) to drive round the block and reverse a little into the top of the Commerce Street exit ramp. Batchelor is now opening the back of the truck to make sure it's clean. A glass soda bottle rolls out and smashes on the floor with a loud bang. A group of reporters run up the ramp to see what's happening. Everyone is jumpy.

'Are you ready?' Chief Curry is asking Captain Fritz.

'We're ready if the security is ready.'

'It's all set up. The people are across the street, and the newsmen are all well back in the basement car park. It's all set. We've got the money wagon up there to transfer him in.'

'Well, I don't like the idea, Chief, of transferring him in a money wagon. We don't know the driver, nor anything about the wagon. It could be used against Oswald by the prosecution in a trial, as we don't usually transport prisoners in an armoured truck. If someone tries to seize Oswald we need to be able to manoeuvre, and that's not easy with such a cumbersome vehicle...'

Curry can see he has a point, and suggests instead that

Oswald is transferred in an unmarked car, with the truck acting as a decoy.

'If anyone planned to try to take our prisoner away from us, they would be attacking an empty armoured car...'

Ruby has parked across the street from the Western Union office, just one block away from City Hall, leaving Sheba in the unlocked car. He's filling out the forms to send the $25 to Karen Carlin. In his pockets are a Colt Cobra .38, and just over $2,000 in cash. It's not unusual for him to carry that much money, and he often carries a gun.

Fritz is trying to persuade Curry to get rid of the television lights and camera crews, who might get in the way of the transfer and also aggravate Oswald with their questions. Curry reassures Fritz that the press is safely behind the rail that divides the ramp and the car park, and then he leaves.

CBS News will record the transfer and then replay it later, as they are concentrating on the events in Washington. At the moment, their reporter Bob Huffaker is in the basement garage, providing commentary to accompany the pictures from their three cameras. Huffaker is good friends with Sergeant Pat Dean, who's been coordinating the security in the basement for the past few hours, so he is well informed.

'Strict security precautions have been exercised from the very beginning and have even been increased this morning, as fear arises and grows stronger that someone may attempt to take the life of the man accused of murdering the president of the United States...'

NBC News director Fred Rheinstein is on the phone to his producer Chet Hagan back in New York, trying to persuade him to take live pictures of Oswald leaving City Hall.

'Chet, this is the last time you're ever going to see this guy. When he gets out of this Keystone Kops situation, they're going to put him in the county jail, the Feds are going to have him, and then he's going to be treated like a regular person with rights. You gotta see him now!' Hagan agrees. NBC will be the only network with live pictures of the transfer.

Fritz tells Detective CN Dhority that the armoured car won't now carry Oswald. He gives him the keys to his car and tells him to park on the ramp as close as he can to the basement jail office. Concerned that someone may try to snatch Oswald, he asks Detective Jim Leavelle to handcuff himself to the prisoner throughout the transfer.

11.12am

Some of the clothing that had been confiscated from Oswald's rooming house in North Beckley has been brought into Fritz's office for the prisoner to change into. With the help of Detective Leavelle and Detective LC Graves, he's putting on a black sweater over his white T-shirt. Fritz asks if he'd like to wear a hat, but Oswald says no.

11.17am

Ruby is handing $30 in notes to Doyle Lane, the Western Union clerk, to pay for the transfer. Lane gives him his change and a receipt stamped '1963 Nov 24 AM 11.17'. He then watches Ruby leave and turn left towards City Hall.

Secret Service agent Forrest Sorrels is telling Fritz that they shouldn't be transporting Oswald so publicly. Fritz says that Curry will never agree to another change of plan.

At the county jail about 2,000 people are on the sidewalks waiting for Oswald to arrive.

11.19am

Chief Curry is on the phone to Mayor Cabell, who's called to check that the transfer is progressing smoothly.

In Fritz's office, Detective Leavelle is fixing handcuffs to Oswald's right wrist and to his own left wrist.

'Lee, if anybody shoots at you, I hope they're as good a shot as you are.' Leavelle jokes, meaning that they'd hit Oswald, and not him.

'Oh, you're being melodramatic. Nobody's gonna shoot at me...' Oswald laughs. Leavelle puts on a wide-brimmed hat that matches his tan suit.

> *I had the gun in my right hip pocket, and impulsively...*
> *I saw him, and that is all I can say. And I didn't care*
> *what happened to me.*
>
> **Jack Ruby Testimony to the Warren Commission**
> **7th June 1964**

11.20am

Handcuffed to Leavelle and with Graves holding his left arm, Oswald is coming out of Fritz's office. Ike Pappas, who's been waiting for his scoop, runs forward with a microphone.

'Do you have anything to say in...' Pappas is thrown against the wall as Oswald is led into the elevator. Pappas dashes for the stairwell and runs down as fast as he can, grateful he'd rehearsed it, and also amazed that there isn't anyone stopping him.

In the basement, the officer in charge of the jail office, Lieutenant Woodrow Wiggins, is watching the elevator lights count down.

In the NBC TV truck, director Fred Rheinstein hears the sound of the elevator picked up by their microphones.

Jack Ruby has stopped at the top of the narrow Main Street ramp leading down to the City Hall basement, joining a small crowd that's gathered there. The Main Street ramp is guarded by patrolman Roy Vaughn, who hears someone at the bottom of the ramp shout, 'Watch that car!' and he turns and sees Lieutenant Rio Pierce, red lights flashing on the grille of his car, coming towards him at speed. Pierce's job is to drive in front of the armoured truck, but as it's blocking the exit, he's going the wrong way up the entrance ramp. As Vaughn steps to one side, and looks east down Main Street to check the road is clear, Jack Ruby slips past him. All his life he's been a gate-crasher, even as a kid, managing to get himself and his friends into baseball games.

Jimmy Turner, a director for WBAP-TV, sees a stocky man in a dark suit and hat walking down the entrance ramp.

The elevator doors are opening and Captain Fritz steps out first, followed by Leavelle, Oswald and Graves.

'Let me have it! I want it!' NBC reporter Tom Pettit shouts to his director.
     NBC News cuts live to Dallas.

The prisoner and escorts are pausing outside the jail office.

'Are they ready?' Fritz says to Lieutenant Wiggins.

'Security is all right,' he replies.

Ike Pappas tumbles out of the stairwell just in time to see Oswald walking past the jail office towards him. He finds a good spot and sticks his elbows out to keep others away.

'Here he comes!' someone shouts.

Jack Ruby sidles in next to CBS cameraman George Phenix in the front of the press line.

11.21am

Captain Fritz is going first, stepping through the doorway that leads from the jail office out into the car park. He's amazed at what he sees. The press, who he'd expected to be on the other side of the ramp rail, are very close. And they surge even closer – officers are struggling to keep them back. The unmarked blue sedan to carry Oswald is further away than Fritz would like.

Leavelle has paused for a second by the doorway.

'Is it okay?' he asks the detective standing just outside.

'Okay, come on out, Jim.'

Leavelle, Oswald and Graves are blinded by the television lights as they emerge.

Ike Pappas is broadcasting live on WNEW-News.

'Now the prisoner, wearing a black sweater – he's changed from his T-shirt – is being moved out toward an armoured car.'

As he reverses towards the jail office in the blue sedan, Detective CN Dhority sounds his horn to get the press to move out of the way.

'There's the prisoner,' says Pappas.

Fritz reaches the sedan. 'Put him in the rear of the car...'

Pappas steps towards Oswald holding his microphone, repeating the question he asked on the third floor.

'Do you have anything to say in your defence...?'

Photographer Bob Jackson is looking through his lens. Suddenly a man steps in front of him, blocking his view. Jackson leans over to the left against the bumper of the police car and presses the shutter.

Detective Leavelle, cuffed to Oswald, recognises Jack Ruby. Ruby is holding a gun.

Arm straight, he presses the barrel against Oswald's chest and pulls the trigger. The bullet goes through Oswald's, spleen, pancreas, aorta, kidney and liver. His groan is heard by the millions watching and listening live.

As Oswald falls to the ground, Ruby lunges forward to shoot again.

Detective Graves grabs Ruby's gun arm with both hands and bends it over his leg. He can feel Ruby squeezing the trigger again.

'Turn it loose! Turn it loose!' Graves shouts.

Ruby drops the gun as five policemen jump on top of him. One has him by the head.

'I hope I killed the son of a bitch!' he says, face pressed to the floor. Several officers have their guns drawn.

As he hurdles over the bonnet of Brown's car to join in the fight, Sergeant Pat Dean thinks, 'My God – a cop has killed him!'

Ike Pappas shouts, 'There's a shot! Oswald has been shot! Oswald has been shot! A shot rang out. Mass confusion here, all the doors have been locked.'

'I'll knock you on your ass!' Detective Dick Swain is shouting as he pushes the press back.

'Nobody out! Nobody out!' Captain Talbert calls to the officers guarding the top of the Main Street and Commerce Street ramps.

Bob Huffaker of CBS recognised the sound of the gun. He used a Colt Cobra when he was a reserve policeman. He thinks Oswald should survive – he once investigated a man who'd been hit by a bullet from a .38, but was still able to beat up the man who shot him.

American television has just filmed its first live murder.

11.22am

Ruby and Oswald are both lying on the floor of the jail office. Leavelle is taking the handcuffs off Oswald, who's groaning.

Ruby is face up, with an officer kneeling on his chest, while another puts handcuffs on him.
　'Who is this son of a bitch?' someone asks.
　'I'm Jack Ruby! You all know me! I'm Jack Ruby!' he says in bewilderment.

Detective Billy Combest lifts up Oswald's sweater and sees that the wound is a serious one.

'Is there anything you want to tell me?' he asks.

Oswald looks at him and shakes his head.

'Is there anything that you want to tell us now?'

Oswald's eyes are closing.

'Is there anything you want to tell me...?'

A white ambulance from Oneal's Funeral Home is on its way.

11.23am

Washington Star reporter Jerry O'Leary managed to slip through the police cordon in the basement, and has made his way up to the third floor. He sees Chief Curry in his office, still on the phone to the Mayor.

'Oswald's been shot,' he says. Curry goes white.

Ruby is being led past Oswald on his way to the elevator and the fifth-floor jail.

'I hope I killed the son of a bitch! It'll save everybody a lot of trouble! Do you think I'm going to let the man who shot our president get away with it?'

Frederick Bieberdorf, a 25-year-old medical student and the first-aid attendant on duty at the jail, is trying to find Oswald's pulse. He can't find one. He tries to hear if he's breathing, but with all the noise in the basement, it's hard to tell. Bieberdorf can see an entry wound between Oswald's ribs, but no sign of external bleeding. He then touches the right side of Oswald's chest, and can feel the bullet still inside him. He starts cardiac massage.

As he travels up in the elevator, Ruby is feeling a sense of relief.

11.24am

Ike Pappas overhears some policemen talking, and sticks his microphone in the middle of them.

'Who is he?' he asks.

'Jack Ruby is the name. He runs the Carousel Club.'

'The Carousel Club!' Pappas exclaims.

'He handed me a card the other day,' another out-of-town reporter says.

Pappas gets out the card Ruby gave him on Friday night and shows the policemen.

'Jack Ruby... is this him?'

'That's him!'

Ruby is upstairs on the fifth floor being searched for weapons; whatever the police find (like $2,000 in notes) is being tossed into his hat. They make him strip down to his boxer shorts.

'Jack, I think you killed him,' Detective Don Archer says.

'Well, I intended to shoot him three times. If I had planned this I couldn't have had my timing better. It was one chance in a million,' Ruby replies, looking Archer right in the eye.

'I guess I just had to show the world that a Jew has guts.'

11.25am

'Here is young Oswald now. He is being hustled in, he is lying flat. He... to me he appears dead. There is a gunshot wound in his lower abdomen. He is white.'

As Oswald is put in the back of the Oneal ambulance, Ike Pappas is continuing his radio commentary.

'Dangling... his head is dangling over the edge of the stretcher...'

At the Parkland Hospital, administrator Peter Geilich has grabbed Major Smith of the Texas Rangers (who are guarding a slowly recovering Governor Connally) and is telling him that Oswald has been shot and there's only one Ranger guarding the Emergency Room. Geilich's assistant, Bill Stinson, over-hears and thinks he's joking, and punches him playfully, but hard, in the stomach, saying 'Be quiet!' Then he sees Geilich is serious and apologises to his boss for punching him.

11.28am

The Executive Inn Motel is very quiet and it's clear to Robert Oswald and translator Peter Gregory that Marguerite was exaggerating when she complained about press intrusion. But she and Marina seem lonely, so Robert is sticking with his plan to move them to the farm in Boyd.

Robert has paid the bill and is walking to his car. Secret Service agent Mike Howard is waiting for him.

'Now, don't get excited, Robert, but we've just heard on the radio that Lee's been shot. It isn't serious, and they've captured the man who shot him.' Robert stays calm only because Howard is.

'Where are they taking him?'

'Parkland Hospital.'

Robert jumps in his car and asks Howard to take his mother and sister-in-law to the farm, and not to tell them or Peter Gregory about the shooting. He's convinced that the entire family is a target for people out for revenge.

Sheriff Decker is standing in front of the county jail in Dealey Plaza and shouting to the hundreds waiting outside.

'Ladies and Gentlemen, Lee Harvey Oswald has been shot and is on his way to Parkland Hospital.'

Hats are waved in the air, and there are loud cheers and applause.

In the ambulance, Oswald has on an oxygen mask, and Fred Bieberdorf is still giving him cardiac massage. Suddenly Oswald comes to, thrashing about as if to stop Bieberdorf, and trying to pull his mask off. A few blocks from Parkland, he stops.

11.32am

The ambulance is pulling up at speed outside the hospital. The police are waiting, as are scores of photographers and reporters. Detective Leavelle runs in first, followed by Oswald on a stretcher, and then by what seems, to the Parkland staff, to be a solid wall of reporters and camera crews.

One of the medical team says that it would be inappropriate for Oswald to go to Trauma Room One where the president died (now with a posy of flowers on the door) and so Oswald is wheeled into Trauma Room Two.

Dr Malcolm Perry, who had treated the dying president only two days before, runs into the Trauma Room. He can see Oswald is unconscious and blue from lack of oxygen, and quickly ascertains that he has no blood pressure and is breathing very weakly. The anaesthetist Dr Marion Jenkins, who also treated Kennedy, puts an endotracheal tube down Oswald's throat to help him breathe.

Dr Tom Shires, the chief of surgery who helped save Governor Connally, arrives to take charge.

11.38am/12.38pm EST

Clint Hill is in his boss Jerry Behn's office when a call comes in for him from General McHugh, President Kennedy's Air Force aide.

'Clint, I'm in the mansion and we have a problem. You'd better get over to the East Room fast. Mrs Kennedy wants to open the casket.'

Hill runs out of the office and finds McHugh standing with Jackie and Robert, both dressed in black.

'Bobby and I want to see the president.'

'All right, Mrs Kennedy. Let me make sure everything is okay.'

Hill last saw the president's body after the autopsy, and he has no idea how it looks after Gawler's men have done their work. McHugh goes to the officer in charge of the Deathwatch honour guard and asks them to leave the room to give Mrs Kennedy some privacy. She interrupts him.

'No, just have the men turn around They can stay where they are. Just have them move away a little.'

Hill and McHugh open the casket. The president looks peaceful. Hill, very relieved, steps aside. Jackie and Robert walk up to the casket and look inside; then after a few moments she says, 'Mr Hill, will you get me a pair of scissors?' He heads off to the chief usher's room, gets some and gives them to Jackie. Hill walks a few feet away and keeps his back turned, but he can hear the snip of the scissors. Jackie then puts in the casket the letter she had written to Jack the night before, a letter from Caroline, a scribbled note from John Jr, a scrimshaw (an engraved whale tooth), and a pair of cufflinks she'd given him. Robert puts in a PT-109 tie clip and a silver rosary.

> *As soon as we got in the car Mr. Gregory says, 'We are taking you to Robert's mother-in-law's house.' Now, they live out in Boyd, Tex, in the country... in a little farmhouse. They are dairy people, Robert's in-laws. And I said, 'No, you are not taking me out in the sticks. I want to be in Dallas where I can help Lee.' 'Well, for security reasons, this is the best place,' he said. I said, 'Security reasons? You can give security for me in a hotel room in town...'*
>
> **Marguerite Oswald testimony to the Warren Commission**
> **10th February 1964**

At the Executive Inn, Marguerite Oswald, still unaware that Lee has been shot, is arguing with Peter Gregory and the agents assigned to her. She's wearing her nurse's uniform – one of the few items of clothing she has with her. Robert had driven off without saying where he was going and she wants to see Lee at the county jail. When they tell her that they are going to the farm in Boyd, she refuses to go. Peter Gregory is furious with her.

'You badgered me to come out and help you, to find you somewhere safe – and here I am! If you don't like this option, then I'm through with helping you!'

Marguerite doesn't argue; she packs her things and gets in the agents' car.

11.39am

Secret Service agent Forrest Sorrels is standing in front of Jack Ruby, who is still wearing only his boxer shorts.

'I want to ask you some questions,' Sorrels says.

'Is this for the magazine or press?' Ruby replies innocently.

Eva Grant, Jack Ruby's sister, has had the television on all morning with the sound down low. She'd seen reruns of the

Oswald shooting on NBC. Its reporter Tom Pettit called the gunman 'Jack Loby', so she suspects nothing. Her phone rings – it's her friend Madeline Blainey.

'How do you feel?' Madeline says.

'Fine.'

'Who is there?'

'Who should be here?'

'Eva, I don't want to be the one who tells you this. Do you know who shot Oswald?'

'No.'

'Jack shot Oswald.'

Eva drops the phone. Then there's knocking on her door.

11.40am

As he drives to Parkland, a stunned Robert Oswald is trying to work out how on earth his brother could have been shot. By now Lee should be in the county jail, so he reckons he must have been shot in his jail cell by a sniper. Nothing else makes sense.

Ruby has just listed to Forrest Sorrels the reasons why he killed Oswald – to save Mrs Kennedy appearing at a trial, the letter to Caroline and his love of the president. His eyes are full of tears.

'I guess I had worked myself into a state of insanity to where I had to do it. I guess I just had to show the world that a Jew has guts.'

'Was anyone involved with you in the shooting of Oswald?' asks Sorrels.

'No, there is no acquaintance or connection between Oswald and myself.'

11.45am

Oswald is now in a second-floor operating theatre at Parkland. Three of the doctors who tried to save Kennedy's life are trying to save the life of his assassin. In all there is a medical team of 11 working to stop the massive blood loss that is killing Oswald.

The bullet is retrieved from just below Oswald's skin and the doctors give it to Jim Leavelle, who has never left this prisoner's side. Leavelle realises that the bullet came close to passing through Oswald and hitting him.

11.46am/12.46pm EST

In the East Room, Robert Kennedy is closing the casket. It is never opened again.

Clint Hill returns the scissors to the chief usher's office. As he puts then in the drawer, he notices a strand of chestnut-coloured hair still attached.

11.47am

Eva Grant wants someone she can trust to get her into City Hall to see her brother. She's calling her favourite weatherman – Jim Underwood of Channel 4 (although they've never met). He promises to pick her up from her apartment.

11.50am/12.50pm EST

In the White House, Clint Hill walks past a group of the household staff. He hears one say, 'That bastard deserved to die'.

'What did you say?!' Hill explodes, thinking they're talking about Kennedy. They explain what's happened to Oswald, but

Hill has no time to take it in, as Mrs Kennedy is about to leave the White House.

12.00pm/1.00pm EST

Jackie Kennedy, in a simple black suit, is standing with the children, both dressed in matching light blue coats, at the top of the steps of the North Portico of the White House. They are watching the casket leave the White House, carried by Lieutenant Sam Bird's military pall-bearers. Television viewers can see that her eyes are puffy with crying. There is an eerie silence, except for the sound of hooves stamping on the ground, from the three pairs of greys that will pull the gun carriage to the Capitol where the president will lie in state. There is a rider on the left-hand horse of each pair, but the saddle on the right-hand horse is empty, to symbolise a fallen leader.

The family and the Johnsons get into a black limousine with Bill Greer at the wheel. John Jr jumps up on the seat and peers out of the window. In front of them, the gun carriage slowly moves away.

12.05pm/1.05pm EST

The muffled drums of the military drum corps leading the cortege echo around Pennsylvania Avenue.

Travelling in a car behind Jackie Kennedy, Clint Hill is scanning the crowd. He's never seen anything like it before – 300,000 silent people, barely moving, many in tears. He watches ex-military men snap to attention as they pass.

Following the gun carriage is Black Jack, a 17-year-old gelding with no rider, and a pair of boots in his stirrups, turned backwards as a further sign that a leader will ride no more. He's making his handler, Private Arthur Carlson, rather nervous, as Black Jack has broken into a sweat, his eyes are rolling and he's becoming very difficult to control. (Black Jack will participate in the funerals of two more presidents, Herbert Hoover and Lyndon Johnson.)

Robert Kennedy watches Carlson struggle with the horse. Jackie says to the new president, 'Oh, Lyndon, what an awful way for you to come in.'

12.10pm/1.10pm EST

Jack Ruby is in his cell, changing into the jail's regulation white shirt and white trousers. Assistant District Attorney Bill Alexander walks in.

'Goddam it, Jack. What did you do this for?'

'Well, you guys wouldn't do it. Someone had to do it. That son of a bitch killed my president!'

As they talk, Alexander realises that Ruby is convinced that he'll soon be released – after all, how angry can you get with the guy who just killed the president's assassin? He really believes he's a hero.

Reporters and photographers are allowed to walk at the rear of the procession to the Capitol. Many in the crowd think they're members of the public and they can join them. As the procession passes Ninth and Pennsylvania, thousands push past the police lining the sidewalks, and start to walk in the procession.

12.20pm

Robert Oswald has reached Parkland Hospital, and has been sitting in his car for 20 minutes. He was stopped at a police cordon and told to wait. Finally two Secret Service agents come out of the hospital, ask him to get out of his car and frisk him for a weapon.

'If only security had been this tight at City Hall,' Robert thinks.

12.30pm/1.30pm EST

Marines with fixed bayonets are now lined up across Pennsylvania Avenue, stopping the crowd from walking further with the procession.

At the Parkland Hospital, administrator Peter Geilich is writing 'PARKLAND' on the blackboard of the classroom that has once again been turned into a temporary pressroom, as some of the out-of-town and foreign press still have no idea of its name. Many of the journalists, like NBC's Robert MacNeil, are finding being back in this room a surreal experience.

12.40pm/1.40pm EST

As Robert Kennedy's car passes the Old Senate Office Building he looks up and says, 'That was where it all began. That was were he ran for the presidency.'

Lady Bird Johnson doesn't know if it's to himself or to John Jr and Caroline that he's speaking.

An agent comes into the Hospital Volunteers room where Robert Oswald is waiting anxiously for news of his brother.

The agent tells him that Lee's injuries aren't serious and 'he's doing fine'. Robert sighs with relief.

12.50pm/1.50pm EST

After a 45-minute journey from the White House, the procession has reached the Capitol. A 21-gun salute begins, the cue for the Navy Band to play a mournful version of 'Hail to the Chief'. Jackie Kennedy bows her head and weeps. The casket is lifted slowly from the gun carriage and carried by the eight-man honour guard into the Rotunda under the giant dome of the Capitol, where members of the House, Senate and Cabinet stand waiting. It's placed in the exact spot and on the same bier where President Lincoln lay in state 98 years before, after his assassination. Television viewers see John Jr gaze upwards at the dome above his head, and Caroline looking only at her mother and the casket.

12.55pm

Secret Service agent Mike Howard is driving Peter Gregory, Marguerite, Marina and the children to Chief Curry's house. They were going to the farm in Boyd until Marguerite insisted that they go first to Ruth Paine's house to pick up diapers for the children. But Howard was warned on the radio that the place is surrounded by reporters, and that they should go instead to Curry's house nearby, where they can call Ruth Paine and arrange for agents to collect the diapers.

But Howard realises that when they go in the house there may be a television or radio on, and they'll find out what's happened to Lee. He turns round and says bluntly to Marguerite, 'Your son has been shot.'

'How badly?' Marguerite asks, shocked.

'In the shoulder.'

Oswald is having a cardiac arrest. Dr Malcolm Perry slices open his chest with a scalpel, reaches in, and starts to massage his heart. A defibrillator repeatedly gives Oswald electric shocks.

1.02pm/2.02pm EST

In the Rotunda of the Capitol and bathed in harsh television lights, the eulogies begin. Senate Majority Leader Mike Mansfield is first. Earlier he'd rehearsed what he wanted to say out loud to his office mirror, but kept breaking down, crying.

President Kennedy, he says, 'gave that we might give of ourselves, that we might give to one another until there was no room, no room at all, for the bigotry, the hatred, the prejudice and the arrogance which converged in that moment of horror to strike him down.'

John Jr is getting restless – he's moving his hands through the air like a jet plane and making engine noises. Jackie nods to agent Bob Foster, who takes John Jr into a side room. As the door closes John Jr says, 'Mr Foster, what happened to my Daddy?'

Foster crouches down to the little boy's level and does his best to explain why his father hadn't come home in his helicopter as he usually did.

For Jackie, Mike Mansfield's eulogy captures the horror of Friday. When Mansfield finishes he walks over to Jackie and gives her the page of his notes.

'You anticipated me,' she says, 'how did you know I wanted it?'

He bows his head.

'I didn't. I just wanted you to have it.'

Nanny Maud Shaw has joined Bob Foster and John Jr, who's noticed a large board covered in miniature flags of the world.

'Please may I have one for my Daddy?' John Jr asks. Maud says that he can, and he chooses a blue one with yellow stars – almost identical to the Presidential flag. It will be buried with his father the following day.

1.07pm

A cardiac pacemaker has been attached by Dr Perry to Oswald's right ventricle. But there is no pulse, no respiratory effort, and his pupils are fixed and dilated.

Dr Jenkins tells them it's over.

Lee Harvey Oswald is pronounced dead.

1.10pm/2.10pm EST

At the foot of the Capitol steps, Jackie Kennedy is standing with the new first lady.

'Lady Bird, you must come back to see me soon, and we'll talk about you moving in.'

'Now there's one thing I want to say about that – I can go and wait till whenever you're ready.'

'Anytime after tomorrow. I won't have anything to do after that,' Jackie replies.

Outside the operating theatre, Peter Geilich is eager for news, as the press are hassling him for an update. The surgery team comes out and tells him that Oswald is dead. Geilich wonders who would be best to brief the press. Dr Malcolm Perry is his first thought, but his briefing after Kennedy's death had been gruelling for him and confusing for the press, so Geilich asks Dr Tom Shires.

Shires agrees, then looks at the huge amount of blood on his surgical scrub suit and disappears to the locker room to get a lab coat to cover it.

1.16pm/2.16pm EST

The eulogies over, tears are running down Robert Kennedy's face. Jackie realises that the short ceremony is finished and everyone is waiting for her to leave first. She turns to Robert, 'Can I say goodbye?'

He nods, and Jackie says to Caroline, 'We're going to say goodbye to Daddy and we're going to kiss him goodbye and tell Daddy how much we love him and how much we'll always miss him.'

They walk up, hand in hand, and as she kneels, Jackie steadies herself on the casket. Caroline looks at her mother to see what she should do.

'You know, just kiss,' Jackie says, and they both kiss the flag-covered casket.

1.20pm

Bob Jackson is arriving at the *Dallas Times Herald* building, having been detained at City Hall for two hours, along with the other press. He can see the chief photographer John Mazziotta waiting outside for him, desperate to get the roll of film developed. They go upstairs to the newsroom where everyone is gathered round a picture taken by Jack Beers of their rival paper the *Dallas Morning News*. It shows the moment just before Jack Ruby shoots. He's stepping forward, gun raised. On the left is a line of plain-clothes policemen; on the right, reporters in raincoats are holding their microphones out to Oswald. No one is looking at the man in the dark suit and hat with a gun – all eyes are on Oswald, striding between detectives Leavelle and Graves.

'Do you have anything this good?' someone says to Jackson.

'I'll let you know in a minute' he replies, coolly. Jackson knows he missed out on a major scoop when he saw the rifle at the sixth-floor depository window, but had no film to capture it. This roll of film might redeem him.

When Mac Kilduff had announced the death of President Kennedy to the press, the room had been quiet and the reporters respectful. Two days later, the atmosphere is very different. Radio and television reporters are crowding around a shocked and hesitant Dr Tom Shires.

'Am I going to answer any questions...?' he says turning to the hospital administrator.

'Speak louder, Doctor!'

'Move forward, Doctor!'

'Is he alive?' shouts a reporter, who can't wait for Shires to read his written statement.

'No. He has died,' Shires replies.

'When did he die, Doctor?'

'He died 1.07 our time, of his gunshot wounds...'

'Did you first inform his relatives of the death before you came here?'

'No, I came right here from the operating room, escorted from the operating room...'

1.24pm

Mike Howard is listening to a message on his radio. Marina

and Peter Gregory are in Chief Curry's house. Marguerite, alone in the back seat of the car, can't quite make it out.

'Do not repeat! Do not repeat!' Howard says urgently.

But Marguerite can now guess what the message is.

'My son is gone, isn't he?'

Howard doesn't answer.

'Answer me! I want to know! If my son is gone, I want to meditate.'

'Yes, Mrs Oswald, your son has just...expired.'

For Marina, Chief Curry's house is an oasis of calm in a day of nightmares. His wife has been kind from the moment she arrived, bringing Marina a glass of water and allowing her to use the phone. Marina walks around admiring the beautiful décor. She's spoken to Ruth, who is sorting out diapers and clothes for the children, and bringing Lee's wedding ring he left behind on Friday morning.

When Marina walks into the sitting room, the television is on and she can tell something is wrong.

'Marina, get a hold of yourself. He's dead,' Peter Gregory says in Russian.

Marguerite comes in, sobbing.

'Marina, our boy is gone...'

The phone rings in the Hospital Volunteers room where Robert Oswald is waiting. John Howlett, the agent with him, answers, listens for about 30 seconds and then says, 'Would you repeat that?' Robert looks up; something in Howlett's tone troubles him. Howlett listens for a few more seconds and hangs up.

'Robert, I'm sorry, but Lee is dead.'

Robert slumps back in his chair and begins to cry for his brother.

As Dr Tom Shires leaves the press conference, WP-BAP reporter Charles Murphy turns to camera.

'This final development – Lee Oswald has died, a fantastic new development in one of the most fantastic stories in American history...'

'DIED 1.07pm' is written in chalk behind him.

> *I remember... taking a good look at Oswald's brother. He was a slender man wearing grey unpressed pants, with matching coat lying on the table. He was wearing a white shirt but no tie. He seemed a nice enough fellow.*
> *Oswald's mother was a rather short woman, about 5'2", quite large and dressed in a white uniform. I thought that this might be a disguise to get her into the hospital area... but I learned later that she works as a practical nurse. I saw Oswald's wife, rather plain, but attractive young girl... [she] had a look of shock about her. The look on her face not unlike that on Mrs Kennedy's face two days earlier.*
>
> *Peter Geilich statement to the FBI*
> *26th November 1963*

1.26pm

Peter Geilich is surprised that the door to the Hospital Volunteer's office is unlocked. He walks in, identifies himself to a Secret Service agent and walks over to Robert Oswald.

'Do you want to talk to the press?' Geilich asks.

'No, no, not at this time...' Robert sobs.

In Chief Curry's house, Mike Howard and other Secret Service agents are watching television replays of Oswald being shot. The set has been turned round so that Marina and Marguerite can't see it.

1.30pm

In the line-up room in the basement of City Hall, Chief Curry is waiting for the reporters to settle, and for the television cameras to get into position.

'My statement will be very brief. Oswald expired at 1.07pm.'

'He died?' one reporter says, incredulous.

'He died at 1.07pm. We have arrested a man. The man will be charged with murder.'

'Who is it?'

'The suspect's name is Jack Rubenstein, I believe. He goes by the name of Jack Ruby. That is all I have to say.'

As he leaves the room, Curry ignores reporters' shouted questions.

Robert Oswald is waiting for the hospital chaplain Kenneth Pepper to arrive so they can pray together, when Secret Service Inspector Thomas Kelley walks in, looks at Robert and says bluntly, 'Violence breeds violence.'

'Does that justify anything in all this?' Robert replies, stunned.

Kelley says nothing and walks out.

2.00pm

Bob Jackson is in the *Dallas Times Herald*'s darkroom. Slowly, an image is appearing. He can see Detective Leavelle leaning back and staring at a man with a gun pressed against Oswald's stomach. Oswald's mouth is open, his eyes closed, his left arm drawn up instinctively across his chest.

'I've got something good!' Jackson shouts.

He will win a Pulitzer Prize for his picture.

2.05pm

'I have a great deal of admiration for police officers. They just did what they had to do. They didn't injure me any more than I'd expect in a scuffle like that.'

Jack Ruby is talking to Frederick Bieberdorf, the jail's first-aid attendant, as he examines his cuts and bruises.

'The police were just doing their job and they did their job well.'

2.30pm/3.30pm EST

Almost every branch of government is involved in some way with the funeral arrangements for Monday. Even the CIA has agreed that its printing presses will work overnight to get the orders of service produced in time. Few in the White House knew that the CIA even had their own press.

Jackie Kennedy, sitting in the West Sitting Room that has become her base, has had an idea.

'There's going to be an eternal flame.'

This is met by a stunned silence. She can see that everyone in the room suddenly looks uncomfortable.

'We'll have to find out if there's one at the Tomb of the Unknowns, because if there is, we can't have one,' Sargent Shriver says.

'I don't care if there is one there. We're going to have it anyway.'

Sargent perists. 'I want to be sure that you're not subjecting yourself to criticism. Some people might think it's a little ostentatious.'

'*Let* them.'

2.45pm

Robert Oswald is sitting in an office close to the hospital morgue, waiting to see Lee's body, and unable to stop crying. Robert had always felt responsible for his troubled little brother when they were growing up – trying to protect him and buying him presents when he could afford to. Lee used to look up to him.

Marguerite and Marina are brought in, and Robert is shocked to discover that they've already seen Lee's body. No one had thought of taking him.

Dr Earl Rose (the Dallas County medical examiner who tried to stop President Kennedy's body leaving the hospital without an autopsy) had warned Marguerite and Marina before they saw the body that it would not be pleasant.

'All the blood has drained from him, and it would be much better if you saw him after he's fixed up.'

'I am a nurse. I have seen death before. I want to see my son now,' Marguerite replies.

'I want to see Lee, too,' Marina says.

Lee Harvey Oswald's body is lying on a trolley in the X-ray department, surrounded by police officers. His body is covered by a sheet, with only his face, now yellow, exposed. To everyone's surprise, Marina walks up to her husband's body and lifts up his eyelids.

'He cry. His eye wet,' she says.

'Yes,' Dr Rose replies.

Marina wants to see the wound that killed Lee. She starts to lift up the sheet but a doctor grabs her arm. So instead she kisses Lee and touches his cold hand. Marguerite has no intention of touching the body; she just wants to make sure that it really is her son.

As she leaves the room, Marina thinks, 'In Russia this wouldn't have happened. They would have taken better care of him.'

Marguerite turns on the policemen standing round her son's body. 'I think some day you will hang your heads in shame. I happen to know, and know some facts, that maybe this is the unsung hero of this episode. And I, as his mother, intend to prove this if I can.'

3.00pm/4.00pm EST

Following Mrs Kennedy's surprise request for an eternal flame to be in place for the interment the following day, presidential advisor Dick Goodwin is on the phone to an Army officer who thinks the whole idea is impossible to achieve in time. He raises objection after objection, but Goodwin dismisses them all. The officer has one last go.

'She can't light it.'

'Why not?'

'It might go out.'

'Listen,' Goodwin says, 'if you can design an atomic bomb, you can put a little flame on the side of that hill, and you can make it so she can light it.'

Marguerite is telling Robert her theory that Lee was an agent for the US government and should be buried at Arlington Cemetery. Robert has no time for his mother's fantasies.

'Oh, Mother, forget it!' he tells her.

3.15pm

Jack Ruby is in Captain Fritz's office, sitting in the same seat as Oswald did 24 hours before. A judge has just read him the complaint that he is charged with shooting and killing Lee Harvey Oswald with 'malice aforethought'.

Fritz is pressing him about how he recognised Oswald.

'I saw him in the show-up room on Friday night. I knew who I was going for.'

Ruby talks about how his grief led to 'a moment of insanity' and how wonderful the Dallas Police Department is. Part-way through he says, 'Don't hate me, Captain Fritz.'

3.20pm/4.20pm EST

Lieutenant Colonel Bernard G Carroll, an engineer at Fort Myers, is looking through the Washington Yellow Pages for the phone numbers of gas companies.

Parkland assistant administrator Peter Geilich is standing at the morgue door, trying to persuade Dr Earl Rose to let Robert see the body.

'Under no circumstances can anyone see the body again,' he says. He is always a stickler for the rules. The legal requirement for a member of the family to identify the body has already been fulfilled.

3.45pm/4.45pm EST

Having tried lots of gas companies, a repairman at Rockville's Suburban Propane answers the phone to Lieutenant Colonel Carroll. He'd just called into their office on his way to an emergency. When he hears what Carroll's ringing for, he agrees to supply anything that he needs.

4.00pm

'Do you have any comments? Do you have anything to say?' reporters are shouting at the Oswalds as they're bundled into two Secret Service cars. A photographer is almost run over as the cars race out of Parkland. Robert never did get to see his brother's body.

On the crowded third floor of City Hall, a reporter says to Captain Fritz, 'Captain, what excuse is there for letting him get that close?'

'I don't have an excuse,' he replies.

4.45pm

The Inn of the Six Flags is a hotel built on the outskirts of Dallas for people visiting the nearby Six Flags Over Texas theme park. November is out of season, so the inn is deserted. This makes it a perfect location for the Secret Service to keep the Oswald family safe. They're being led to Rooms 423 and 424 at the rear of the building. An agent tells Robert Oswald that the FBI will soon be looking after them, but Robert heard earlier from another agent that the Secret Service will remain their guardians. He senses that something is wrong.

5.05pm

Jack Ruby once helped two police officers who were being attacked in the street by three men armed with beer bottles. Ruby jumped in to even the odds, punching hard. Now he's being fingerprinted by one of those officers – Ed Carlson, who became a friend. Ruby asks after DL Blankenship, the other cop in the fight.

The Police Department is receiving a number of Western Union telegrams for Jack Ruby:

I WOULD BE HONORED TO CALL YOU FRIEND ALICE ROSARIO SAN FRANCISCO.

THANK GOD THERE IS ONE MAN IN AMERICA WHO KNOWS HOW TO DEAL WITH PUNKS THERESA BANNIGAN NEW JERSEY.

WE LOVE YOUR GUTS AND COURAGE CLAYTON T. DODGE MIAMI.

HEARTIEST CONGRATULATIONS FOR A JOB WELL DONE FRANK XINNEY BEVERLY HILLS.

By the end of the day, Ruby will receive over 100 telegrams.

6.00pm

To Robert Oswald, the Inn of the Six Flags looks like an armed camp – agents with rifles circle the hotel and are stationed close to their rooms.

'All we need is to have one or more of you killed or injured, and we're in real trouble,' an agent with little tact tells Robert.

'Jim, now that Oswald is dead, there isn't going to be trial. Here – take these, I don't ever want to see them again.' FBI supervisor Gordon Shanklin is handing James Hosty the 'Hasty' note Oswald wrote demanding he stay away from his wife, as well as a memo that explained the background to it. Shanklin is terrified that J Edgar Hoover will get to hear of their existence. Hosty starts tearing it up.

'No! Not here! I told you I don't want to see them again! Now get them out of here!' Shanklin shouts.

Hosty walks to the nearest men's room, goes into a cubicle, tears the note into smaller pieces and flushes them down the toilet.

> **One of the things that he loved about this President – he didn't care what you were, you were a human being and Jack felt that this was one time in history that Jews are getting the break. He put great Jewish men in office.**
>
> **Eva Grant testimony to the Warren Commission**
> **28th May 1964**

Eva Grant is visiting her brother in jail. He shows her a colour photograph of JFK he keeps in his white prison jacket. Ruby kisses the photograph, rather like a baby, Eva thinks.

6.30pm/7.30pm EST

Despite the cold, thousands of people have been queuing all day to walk past to pay their respects to their dead president. The line now stretches for nine miles through the Washington streets. For those at the back, it will be eight hours before they climb the steps of the Capitol. Once inside, the queue splits in half, with people walking either side of the casket. Some are dressed in their Sunday best, some have come straight from their farms. Some cry into handkerchiefs, some just stare.

The Deathwatch honour guard around the casket, made up of representatives of each the armed services, is changing as it does every half-hour. They will keep their vigil, facing their fallen Commander in Chief, all though the night.

The statues of two assassinated presidents – Abraham Lincoln and James A Garfield – watch from their pedestals.

6.40pm

Secret Service agent Mike Howard is briefing Robert. He's received instructions that the Secret Service is to continue protecting Marina and Marguerite, but there was no mention of him. Howard has been to check if Robert had been deliberately overlooked.

'They've called the president and he has expressed concern for you and the entire family. So has the attorney general.' Robert is touched that Robert Kennedy, in his grief, should be interested in the safety of the family of his brother's killer.

Marina Oswald has received a telegram from a group of American college students. 'We send you our heartfelt sympathy. We understand your sorrow and we share it. We are ashamed that such a thing could happen in our country. We beg you not to think ill of us. You have friends and we are with you.'

The Secret Service is being forwarded hundreds of letters addressed to Marina. None are hostile, and many are offers of help from ordinary members of the public, touched by the plight of the young widow and her children. Some letters come with dollar bills attached. By mid-December Marina will receive over $25,000 through the post.

7.00pm/8.00pm EST

A call is put through to Robert Oswald from the Parkland Hospital, who want to know what they should do with his brother's body. He hasn't even started to think about a funeral. Mike Howard suggests the Miller Funeral Home, run by his friend Paul J Groody, might help.

Almost every bedroom in the White House is being used by the

231

Kennedy and Bouvier families. Jackie's sister Lee Radziwill and her husband Stanislaw have been given the president's bedroom. Stanislaw is looking at the familiar four-poster and Jack's pills on the bedside table, and feeling very uneasy about being here. He can't bear to go into the bathroom, with its toy boats John Jr used for bathtimes with his father. Although Lee is happy to sleep in the four-poster, Stanislaw asks for a camp bed.

White House maid Lucinda Morman is making a black mourning veil for Mrs Kennedy to wear tomorrow, as it's proved to be impossible to buy one.

7.15pm

'I'm not interested in an elaborate casket. But I do want a heavy steel outer vault, which would be safe from vandals,' Robert Oswald says to Paul J Groody, the director of the Miller Funeral Home.

8.00pm/9.00pm EST

Under arc lights at Arlington, Lieutenant Colonel Carroll is coordinating the construction of the eternal flame. A torch welded to a frame has arrived from the Washington Gas and Light Company. Tanks and 300 feet of tubing from Rockville's Suburban Propane are being buried in a trench.

District Attorney Henry Wade went home after Ruby shot Oswald, tired and dispirited. He went to sleep this afternoon and woke up about 5pm to hear someone on the television attack him and the Dallas Police for incompetence. They said that the Dallas Police had arrested the wrong man and allowed Oswald to be killed by Ruby. Incensed, Wade headed to City

Hall and tried to persuade Chief Curry to speak to the press and lay out all the evidence they had against Oswald. Curry said it was a bad idea and that he'd given his word to the FBI not to talk about evidence in public again.

Undeterred, Wade is jotting down in a notebook, from memory, seven key bits of evidence. He will speak to the press, even if Curry won't.

8.10pm

Robert Oswald is eavesdropping.

'Maybe the Feebies don't know where we are!' a Secret Service agent is joking, using their nickname for the FBI. It's clear that the agents had expected to hand over responsibility for the family to the FBI, because guarding the families of dead alleged assassins is not part of their job. Robert has heard stories that his brother was part of a conspiracy; he wonders if the Secret Service suspect that the FBI were somehow in on it, and therefore can't be trusted.

8.30pm/9.30pm EST

Robert Kennedy, Jackie Kennedy and her sister Lee are finishing their supper in the family sitting room of the White House. Robert goes downstairs to join the rest of the family and the house guests in the dining room. Aristotle Onassis, the million-aire ship owner, is being teased about his considerable wealth. Robert joins in, drawing up a mock formal document, stating that Onassis must give half his fortune to the poor of South America. Robert dislikes Onassis, as did JFK (before a trip to Greece in 1961 he'd said to Clint Hill 'don't let Mrs Kennedy cross paths with Aristotle Onassis'), so Jackie's invitation to him to come to the funeral took many people by surprise.

Parkland won't release Oswald's body to the Miller Funeral Home until they are sure that the request is genuine. A complicated way to check the authenticity of the request has been set up. Parkland have given the Dallas Police a secret password; they in turn have passed it on to the Secret Service, who have just given it to Robert Oswald. He dials the hospital.

'Malcolm' he says.

'All right,' says the man at the other end.

Malcolm is the name of the surgeon who tried to save both the president's life and his assassin's.

Jackie and Robert Kennedy are being driven once more to the Capitol, so they can kneel and pray by the casket. Many of the people they pass queuing in the cold are singing hymns, spirituals and protest songs.

9.25pm

Using his notebook with its list of seven key pieces of evidence against Oswald, Henry Wade addresses the press and television cameras in the line-up room at City Hall. Some of what he says is accurate, but much is incomplete or simply wrong. He tells them Marina discovered the rifle missing after her husband went to work; that Oswald's gun misfired when he pointed his revolver at McDonald's head in the Texas Theater; that his name was given out soon after Kennedy's murder.

'Would you be willing to say in view of all this evidence that it is now beyond reasonable doubt at all that Oswald was the killer of President Kennedy?'

'I would say that without any doubt he's the killer,' Wade replies.

'As far as you are concerned, the evidence you gave us, you could have convicted him?'

'I've sent people to the electric chair on less.'

'Will you seek the electric chair for Ruby?'

'Yes.'

Within a few minutes of speaking to the press, District Attorney Wade gets a call from the FBI insisting he says nothing more about the case.

9.30pm/10.30pm EST

Rose Kennedy is at the Capitol, kneeling in front of her son's casket. She's thinking of how Mary suffered the pain of looking at her dying son on Calvary, and how she still trusted in God and bore everything patiently. Rose will think of Mary and Calvary five years later, after the shooting of her son Robert – her fourth child to die.

Funeral director Paul J Groody is not having an easy time finding a cemetery that will take the body of Lee Harvey Oswald. Robert is calling round ministers to find one who is happy to officiate at the funeral.

'No, we can't do that,' says one.

'Why not?'

'We can't go along with what you have in mind. Your brother was a sinner.'

Robert hangs up.

The day ends with no minister in place for the funeral the following afternoon.

11.20pm/12.20am EST

In the dark of Arlington Cemetery, Lieutenant Colonel Carroll is about to test the eternal flame for the first time. It works. He tests it again, and again. Each time, he's illuminated by a large, bright orange dancing light.

11.30pm/12.30am EST

A few hundred yards from Lieutenant Colonel Carroll, a strange scene is taking place.

One thing has concerned Lieutenant Sam Bird since he and his honour guard first carried the president's casket – its extreme weight. He is terrified that they will drop it during tomorrow's funeral. That morning he had added two more men to get it up the steps of the Capitol, but even then they'd struggled. It will be even harder bringing it down.

Bird has decided that they must rehearse as best they can. He's borrowed an empty Army casket and some sandbags from Fort Myers and driven over with the honour guard to the Tomb of the Unknowns at Arlington Cemetery.

They've filled the casket with the sandbags and are now carrying it slowly down the steps by the tomb. All this is done silently. There are no commands from Bird; everything is done by a nod of his head.

11.45pm/12.45am EST

Lieutenant Bird doesn't feel the sandbags are heavy enough. The Tomb of the Unknowns has a sentry who marches in front of it all day, but at night he's off duty. Bird has persuaded him to sit on the casket, and the sweating honour guard is now carrying him and the sandbag-filled casket down the tomb's marble steps.

Shortly, Bird himself will join the sentry on the casket.

4.20pm Monday 25th November: The Oswald family by the graveside at Rose Hill Cemetery, Fort Worth.

Monday 25th November 1963

3.15am/4.15am EST

Roy Kellerman is in the Cathedral of St Matthew making sure the location is secure for President Johnson and the Kennedy family. He's not alone – the CIA and FBI are there too, along with police from Scotland Yard, West Germany, France and Japan. After two shootings in three days, the world doesn't trust American security arrangements.

4.45am/5.45am EST

In Pennsylvannia Avenue, the police are telling the people at the back of the queue that the doors to the Capitol will close at 8.30am, they won't get in and they should go home. Over 250,000 people have so far walked past the casket.

6.30am/7.30am EST

Robert Kennedy woke early, feeling restless, and so slipped out of the White House for a brisk walk, to think about the day ahead and what he'll say at his brother's graveside. He's now on his way back down Pennsylvania Avenue but he's being recognised; people are stopping to offer their condolences.

7.00am/8.00am EST

The sun is shining in a blue sky over Washington. It is cold and clear.

Today is John Jr's third birthday and he's opening two presents – a toy helicopter from Caroline and a copy of *The Tale of Peter Rabbit* from Maud Shaw.

8.30am

Paul J Groody calls Robert Oswald to tell him that Rose Hill Cemetery in Fort Worth will let Lee be buried there. Neither of them so far has been able to find a minister prepared to officiate.

9.00am

At Parkland Hospital, a floral spray of white carnations is being hung on the door of Trauma Room One. Hospital chaplain Kenneth Pepper says a prayer and staff and patients watch in silence. Over the next few weeks, Trauma Room One will only be used when absolutely necessary.

NBC reporter Robert MacNeil is on the grassy knoll in Dallas, three days since he was last here, chasing policemen searching for a gunman. He's looking at the flowers that have been placed on the side of the road, some with notes attached.

'To my friend, John F Kennedy' one says, in a child's handwriting.

'God forgive us all.'

'I'm sorry, Caroline and John Jr.'

9.25am/10.25am EST

In an alcove just off the Rotunda, Lieutenant Sam Bird is praying with his casket team.

'Dear God, please give us strength to do this one last thing for the president.'

9.39am/10.39am EST

Walking up the steps of the Capitol are Jackie, veiled and dressed in black, and Robert and Ted Kennedy in dress suit and tails. Clint Hill is a pace behind them. Ted Kennedy's dress suit arrived this morning incomplete, so he's wearing the gloves and trousers JFK wore at his inauguration (which valet George Thomas has let out at lightning speed to fit Ted). Ted had no hat, so Robert decided he wouldn't bother with his. As a result, no other men at the funeral will wear them.

'The stamina of this woman through these past four days has been indescribable. It certainly has touched the entire nation,' says NBC's Chet Huntley.

Jackie, Robert and Ted walk up to the casket, kneel and pray for a minute, and then walk away, not turning their backs to the casket until they have to.

Marina Oswald overheard one of the Secret Service men say that the president's funeral was on television, and she's asked Robert if he would turn it on. Immediately an agent leaps up and turns it off.

'I don't think you should watch this,' he says.

'No, I watch,' and Marina turns it back on. She will watch the coverage continually until she has to leave to go to her husband's funeral.

9.50am/10.50am EST

A military band is playing 'O God of Loveliness', as the casket team walks slowly down the 36 steps of the Capitol. Their night-time rehearsal has paid off – they are carrying it with ease.

In the Oval Room, Kenny O'Donnell, Dave Powers and other Kennedy aides are watching the procession on television. Dave Powers is marching John Jr up and down and getting him to salute to order. Powers suggests that they drink a champagne toast to their dead friend.

'I can see the president in heaven. He's looking down and saying, "Look at that son of a bitch Powers. He can always find an excuse for a toast when it's my liquor he's drinking."'

Joe Kennedy is being taken for a drive by his niece Ann Gargan through towns near his home at Hyannis Port. Joe motions to Ann to slow down, so he can see the shop window displays with pictures of his dead son, many of them surrounded by black crepe.

9.55am/10.55am EST

Sergeant Keith Clark has arrived at Arlington Cemetery for a rehearsal.

He's a Navy bugler and his job will be to play 'Taps' – the tune performed at dusk and at military funerals, also known as 'The Day Is Done'. He had played it at Arlington two weeks earlier on Veterans Day, when the president had visited the Tomb of the Unknowns with John Jr.

Clark can see that a television crew has marked the spot where they want him to stand with a cross of masking tape. To his dismay it's directly in front of the Old Guard, who will fire their traditional three-volley salute just before he has to play. Clark knows he'll be deafened, but for the cameras it'll make an excellent shot. Clark's commanding officer reassures him that it'll all be fine.

10.00am/11.00am EST

Robert Oswald is in his hotel room on the phone to chaplain Kenneth Pepper at Parkland, who's called to see if all the funeral arrangements are in place. Robert tells him about all the negative responses he's had so far.

'It seems to me that there are a lot of hypocrites around. Let's examine the Church's position. After all, was the assassination the act of a sane man?' Robert asks.

'Maybe I can convince some of the ministers by raising that question. They surely would agree that you can't hold an insane person responsible for his acts.'

Pepper begins to make some calls.

In Manhattan, the executives of Time Inc are wrapping up a board meeting. They've just watched Abraham Zapruder's film that Richard Stolley brought up from Dallas over the weekend and paid $50,000 for. CD Jackson, the publisher of *Life,* is so shocked by the sight of Kennedy's head exploding that he proposes that Time buy the film rights and withhold the film from public viewing.

Pipe Major JB Anderson and the eight pipers of the Black Watch Regiment are waiting in front of the White House for the funeral procession to begin. They are watching, wide-eyed, as Lana Turner and Frank Sinatra walk by. Two weeks before, the pipers had played for the president on the White

House lawn, and just as their bus was about to leave, JFK got on. He shook all of them by the hand, and chatted for 15 minutes. This encounter, which the pipers will remember for the rest of their lives, makes this morning's task even more poignant.

10.35am/11.35am EST/4.25pm GMT

The BBC coverage of the funeral is just beginning, with its veteran broadcaster Richard Dimbleby providing the commentary. The programme will last only 30 minutes, stopping just before the Requiem Mass begins, but for *The Times* the following day, 'the linking of the two nations for half an hour by the satellite broadcast was the most poignant time of the long day's ceremony. With this broadcast it was as though the shared grief had truly annihilated space and time.'

The gun carriage bearing the president's casket has arrived at the White House, and the funeral procession is about to begin. The fact that Jackie wants to walk to St Matthew's has created a nightmare scenario for the Secret Service and the other agencies who've flown in to protect some of the most powerful men and women in the world.

Waiting outside the White House are President Johnson, Charles de Gaulle in the uniform of the French Army, the Duke of Edinburgh in his Admiral's uniform, Sir Alec Douglas-Home, Anastas Mikoyan, the Soviet first deputy, Emperor Haile Selassie and other foreign leaders and monarchs.

Marching with them will be 64 CIA agents, 40 FBI agents, 250 State Department security men and 22 security men for de Gaulle alone (who has survived four assassination attempts already).

The bell of St John's Episcopal Church, the 'Church of Presidents', begins to toll. Jackie, her face veiled, starts walking, with her brothers-in-law on either side, as the Black Watch pipers play the funeral tunes they've been rehearsing for the last 24 hours.

Behind Jackie is a limousine carrying her children and Maud Shaw. On each side of the car is a Secret Service agent. Caroline winds down a rear window and reaches out to take the hand of agent Bob Foster. Behind his sunglasses, Foster is trying hard not to cry. She holds his hand all the way to St Matthew's.

President Johnson is hard to see, as he's surrounded by Roy Kellerman and his agents who are scanning the crowd and every window. Most of them haven't slept for four days. Kellerman had asked Johnson not to walk in the open.

'I'd rather give my life than be afraid to give it,' the president had replied.

Behind them is a block of foreign dignitaries and security men stretching right across Pennsylvania Avenue. Following them is Kennedy's Cabinet and the Supreme Court Justices, friends of the family and then White House staff.

As they walk, the Kennedy brothers occasionally say to each other and Jackie, 'This is too fast' or 'A little faster.'

Richard Dimbleby is commentating on the BBC:

'All the time Mrs Kennedy preserves this quiet silent dignity. Many people ask how much longer she can continue...'

Six-year-old Susie Bodrogi steps from the kerb with a dozen red roses in her arms and walks to the middle of the street. As the soldiers and the rest of the cortege march towards her, Susie kneels and calmly lays the roses one by one on the ground, and then returns to her family.

An old man is walking towards Robert MacNeil and his film crew on the grassy knoll in Dealey Plaza. The man turns on a transistor radio, and the sound of the president's funeral echoes around the knoll. When MacNeil hears the bagpipes of the Black Watch, he starts to cry. Just a fortnight before he'd been at the White House watching them play on the South Lawn, as the Kennedy family watched from the balcony.

10.57am/11.57am EST

The gun carriage pulls up outside St Matthew's, and on the steps, waiting to meet the Kennedy family, is the tall figure of Cardinal Cushing, the archbishop of Boston. He married Jackie and Jack, prayed at his inauguration, christened Caroline and John Jr and last August, buried two-day-old Patrick.

The cardinal kisses Caroline, pats John Jr on the head and puts an arm round Jackie.

11.04am

A Lutheran minister, Reverend French, is sitting on a sofa in Robert Oswald's room at the Inn of the Six Flags. He has Robert on one side and Marguerite on the other. He has been told by the local Council of Churches that the family are struggling to find someone to take the funeral service for Lee. French feels very uneasy. He's only really here because the Oswald family is Lutheran. Robert is crying.

French tells them that it is impossible for the president's assassin to have a funeral service in church, as he is a 'lost sheep'.

'Well, if Lee is a lost sheep, and that's why you don't want him to go to church, he's the one that should go into church. Good people do not need to go to church. Let's say he is called a murderer. It's the murderers we should be concerned about,' Marguerite snaps.

A Secret Service agent interrupts.

'Mrs Oswald, be quiet – you're making matters worse.'

Marguerite fumes, but Reverend French agrees to officiate – but at the cemetery chapel, not a church. Before he leaves, the agent, suspecting that the minister is in two minds about it, makes sure he knows how to get to Rose Hill and that the funeral is at 4.00pm.

> *Leon Hubert: [The transfer] was done at an unannounced hour?*
>
> *Well sir, it was so unannounced that the Chief didn't know about it and neither did Sheriff Decker. I don't know whether they will admit that or not, but no one knew it but Captain Fritz and myself and the three or four officers directly involved. I brought Ruby down in safety... I don't think you can argue with success.*
>
> *James Leavelle testimony to the Warren Commission*
> *25th March 1964*

Captain Fritz is at the Greyhound Bus Station in Dallas. He has a plan to restore the reputation of his force. He dials his secretary's number, who puts the call through to Detective Leavelle in the squad room, back on duty after the high drama of yesterday.

'Are you in a position where you can talk?' Fritz asks.

'No, not really, Captain.'

Fritz tells him to use the phone in his office, and when Leavelle picks it up, outlines a plan to transfer Jack Ruby.

'I have Officers Graves and Montgomery with me. We have cased the county jail and it looks clear. I'm going to make a suggestion to you, and if you don't think it will work I want you to tell me. Go get Ruby out of the jail, anyway you want to, and bring him down in the elevator and I'll drive through the basement at a given time, and we'll load Ruby up and whisk him right on down to the county jail with another squad following us. Do you think it will work?'

'Yes, I think it will, the way it's set up.'

'I haven't called Sheriff Decker or Chief Curry about it,' says Fritz.

'All you can do is get a bawling-out, but a bawling-out is better than losing a prisoner,' Leavelle replies enthusiastically. This is the sort of plan he had suggested to Chief Curry on Saturday night for Oswald's transfer.

'Have you got enough men there to help you?' Fritz says.

'Yes, there are three or four here I can get.'

'Don't tell anybody where you are going. Just get them like you are going after some coffee, and when you're downstairs tell them what you are going to do.'

11.10am/12.10am EST

Jackie and the children take their seats in the front row of St Matthew's. It's been a nightmare for Angier Duke, the White House chief of protocol, to find seats for everyone, and a location appropriate to their status. He has not always succeeded, partly because he hasn't allowed extra space for some people wearing overcoats or swords, leaving fewer seats than expected. Princess Beatrix of the Netherlands is in a side chapel with no view of the altar, sandwiched between the Soviet first deputy Anastas Mikoyan and his bodyguard. So they can see what's going on, Angier Duke has found a television set showing the funeral and set that up in the chapel.

Two of the last people to enter the cathedral, just before the doors close, are Dr Martin Luther King and Judge Sarah T Hughes, who swore in Johnson on Air Force One.

The Pontifical Requiem Mass for John F Kennedy begins.

'Introibo ad altare Dei, ad Deum qui lætificat iuventutem meam...' recites Cardinal Cushing. On the three television networks, the Latin is being translated into English: 'I shall go into the altar of God, the God who gives joy to my youth...'

11.12am/12.12pm

Jim Leavelle has recruited Detectives Brown, Dhority and Beck to help him transfer Jack Ruby. Brown and Beck have gone to get a car from the basement car park and will be in position at 11.15am, ready to ride ahead of Fritz's car.

Leavelle is in the jail elevator with Dhority and Ruby, who's dressed in a white prison shirt and white trousers. Leavelle has been going to Ruby's clubs on police business for over a decade.

'Jack, in all the years I've known you, you've never deliberately caused any police officer any trouble that I know of, but you didn't do us any favours when you shot Oswald. You've really put the pressure on us.'

'That's the last thing in the world I wanted to do. I just wanted to be a damn hero and all I've done is foul things up,' Ruby replies.

Leavelle leaves Dhority and Ruby in the elevator, and although Beck is in place with the police car, there's no sign of Fritz. Large television cameras lie abandoned.

Leavelle gets back in the elevator, and Brown keeps the officer in the jail office talking, all the while keeping an eye out for the Captain.

The three men wait in the elevator. It's a bizarre rerun of the previous day's dramatic transfer, almost to the hour. Leavelle can see that Ruby is nervous.

'I don't want to have to push you or shove you. I want you to *move*.'

Brown gives him the nod that Fritz has driven into the basement.

Ruby is so terrified that there may be an assassin waiting for him that he almost outruns Leavelle and Dhority to the car. Ruby dives down on the floor of the back seat, and Leavelle puts his feet on his back. Within a few minutes, having taken the route they'd planned for Oswald, Jack Ruby is in the county jail.

At Jackie's request, Clint Hill is sitting directly behind her. She begins to cry and Hill leans over and gives her a handkerchief that he'd brought just in case.

John Jr is restless and says, 'Where's my Daddy?' and lifts up his arms to be picked up. Agent Bob Foster steps forward and carries him to the back of the cathedral. They sit in an ante-room and Foster tells him made-up stories of Jasper the Jet, as he's done so many times before. This time it doesn't work, so Foster takes a leaflet from a rack and starts telling him stories about Jesus, and John Jr settles down. (In the weeks that follow, John Jr starts calling Foster 'Daddy'.)

11.25am/12.25pm EST

From his bed at the Parkland Hospital, Governor John Connally is watching the funeral on television. His 17-year old son Johnny is representing him at St Matthew's.

Much of the country is watching too – an estimated 175 million television viewers. At Grand Central Terminal in New York, a giant screen has been set up and thousands of commuters are rooted to the spot. No trains are running while the service is taking place. Greyhound buses have parked up, and the New York Subway has stopped.

In Tokyo Bay, Japanese fishing vessels, their flags at half-mast, are drifting alongside US Navy warships in quiet tribute.

The Stars and Stripes that flies over the West Berlin side of Checkpoint Charlie is also at half-mast. To show respect, the guards on the Communist side have taken down the East German flag.

At the Rose Hill Cemetery in Fort Worth, two groundsmen are digging a grave. They've been told it's for a 'William Bobo'.

Jackie, Ted and Robert are kneeling at the chancel rail, receiving Communion from the cardinal.

11.30am

At Beckley Hills Baptist Church, the final preparations are being made for JD Tippit's funeral. A black woman appears at the church door and asks to view the body – an unusual request in segregated Texas. Two policemen walk down the street to Marie Tippit's house and ask if it's all right for the woman to do so.

'By all means, let her in. JD has done something good for her and her family. She just wants to pay her respects.'

11.35am/12.35pm EST

Bishop Philip Hannan, an old friend of JFK climbs into the pulpit, and in his address weaves in some of the president's favourite biblical passages, including from Ecclesiastes:

'There is an appointed time for everything, and a time for every affair under the heavens. A time to be born and a time to die...'

Bishop Hannan ends by reciting in full President Kennedy's

inaugural address. The most famous lines of the Kennedy presidency echo around the cathedral:

'… and so my fellow Americans, ask not what your country can do for you; ask what you can do for your country…'

As he speaks, the bishop remembers how the two of them used to discuss the art of public speaking. The morning after the inaugural address, JFK had rung him and said, 'Well, how did it go?'

'It's a masterpiece, the best inaugural address in one hundred years. But you should have spoken more slowly, to wait for the crowd reaction…'

To *New York Times* reporter Tom Wicker, watching from his pew in the cathedral, the words from the inauguration seem more relevant in the aftermath of Dallas than they did in January 1961 when he first heard them.

11.50am/12.50pm EST

One of Jack Ruby's lawyers is about to leave his cell in the county jail. Joe Tonahill came because he wanted to talk to Ruby to make sure he wasn't part of some wider communist plot – he'd heard some wild stories about his client.

Ruby stands up and shakes Tonahill by the hand.

'Well, Joe, you make a good impression. I'm glad to have you with me!' Tonahill is stunned. Ruby is acting as if he'd been auditioning him to perform at one of his clubs. Tonahill isn't concerned now about any communist plot, rather that Ruby seems divorced from reality and strangely exhilarated by his situation.

The cardinal is circling the flag-covered casket three times, covering it in incense and sprinkling it with holy water. He suddenly breaks from the Latin of the Mass and says in English, 'May the angels, dear Jack, lead you into Paradise! May the martyrs receive you at your coming! May the Spirit of God embrace you, and may you, with all those who made the supreme sacrifice of dying for others, receive eternal rest and peace. Amen.'

To Jackie Kennedy it sounds like a friend's wail of anguish.

'That's all right, you done your best; it's all over now.'

12.10pm/1.10pm EST

The Requiem Mass over, the Kennedy family is at the foot of the steps of St Matthew's. The casket has been placed on the gun carriage and the band are playing 'Hail to the Chief' to the 35th president of the United States for the last time. Men in the crowd are saluting, as are the soldiers on the steps and around the carriage. Jackie whispers something to John Jr and takes from him the leaflet Bob Foster gave him. He steps forward, stands straight, and with his right hand, salutes his father's casket perfectly. It will be one of the most poignant images of the day.

Then there is chaos as the congregation tries to find a car to take them to Arlington Cemetery. Former presidents Eisenhower and Truman, arch rivals for a decade, end up getting in a limousine together; the joint chiefs are kept waiting as they've lost their car to Caroline and John Jr, as their mother decided that they should return to the White House.

In the end, the line of vehicles behind the horse-drawn carriage is three miles long.

12.30pm/1.30pm EST

Lieutenant Bird, in charge of the casket team, hears a lady in the crowd call out to her dead president as they march by, 'That's all right, you done your best; it's all over now.'

1.00pm

Nightclub reporter Tony Zoppi is having lunch at the King's Club in Dallas. The manager tells him that Jack Ruby is on the phone, calling from his jail cell. Zoppi has known Ruby for over a decade. After some small talk Zoppi can't contain himself.

'Jack, why the hell did you do it?'

Ruby starts to cry.

'I didn't want Jackie to have to come down here and stand trial against that commie rat. And those poor kids left without a father. I was raised without a father and I know what they're going through… I've got to tell you something that I've never told anyone.'

Zoppi thinks that he might have a scoop on his hands – he knows Ruby trusts him. Ruby tells him that every Christmas he takes presents to children in an orphanage in Oak Cliff.

'This year nobody is going to get a gift…' He suddenly stops crying and says defiantly, '…and I wanted to prove there was one Jew with guts.'

1.35pm/2.35pm EST

The cortege has taken over an hour to get to Arlington. A million people were on the streets to watch it pass. Now the gun carriage is slowly climbing the path that winds through the trees of the cemetery. The horses are tiring now. As Lieutenant

Sam Bird walks, he has his eyes fixed on the flag that has covered the casket since Bethesda Hospital. He notices a label on it, 'Valley Forge Flag Company, Spring City, Pennsylvania'. He decides to write them a letter to tell them how their flag was used.

1.47pm/2.47pm EST

Standing by the grave, surrounded by thousands of white head-stones, are 39 teenage cadets from the Irish Guard. They have been standing for three hours; when they arrived the grave was still being dug. Never before has a foreign army been asked to take part in the graveside ceremony of an American president.

When JFK visited Ireland in the summer, he'd taken part in a wreath-laying ceremony and had been impressed by the 36th Cadet Class Guards and their Queen Anne drill, performed at funerals and memorial services. When Kennedy returned to Washington, he requested a special film be made of the drill, so he could show others, and watch it whenever he liked.

Jackie, Robert, Ted, the Kennedy sisters Patricia, Eunice, Jean and their mother Rose are being led to seats by the graveside. The family is surrounded, not only by the Irish Cadets, but also by platoons from each of the nation's armed services. The foreign dignitaries and heads of state are still making their own way to the grave; many will only hear snatches of what is said.

On cue, 50 F-105 jet fighters in formation, one for each state, roar overhead. They're followed by the plane that JFK loved most of all – Air Force One. At the controls, and flying at 600mph and only 500 feet, is Colonel Jim Swindal, who dips the wings of the Boeing in salute.

As Air Force One disappears, orders in Gaelic are shouted to the Irish cadets. They start their swift and silent drill with rifles reversed, in honour of the dead president. At one point, the cadets have to stretch out their left arms and look to their left. They find themselves gazing straight at Jackie Kennedy. Then the cadets turn and bow their heads, a final salute to the deceased.

Cardinal Cushing walks up to the grave and begins the committal.

'O God, through whose mercy the souls of the faithful find rest, be pleased to bless this grave and send Thy holy angels to keep it and loose from the bonds of sin the body we bury herein, that of our beloved Jack Kennedy, the 35th president of the United States, that his soul may rejoice in Thee with all the saints, through Christ the Lord, Amen.

'I am the Resurrection and the Life. He who believeth in Me, although he be dead, shall live, and everyone who liveth and believeth in Me, shall not die for ever.'

A gun battery across the cemetery fires a 21-gun salute, as the cardinal sprinkles holy water on the casket.

2.00pm

At Beckley Hills Baptist Church, Marie Tippit sits with her three children, close to the open casket of her husband JD. A police honour guard stands around it. The 400-seat church is full of family and police colleagues. In the Sunday School rooms and outside, 1,000 people watch the service on closed-circuit televisions. It's also being recorded by local Dallas TV stations, so it can be shown after the president's funeral.

'Today we are mourning the passing of a devoted public servant,' the Reverend CD Tipps tells the congregation. 'He was doing his duty when he was taken by the lethal bullet of a poor, confused, misguided, ungodly assassin – as was our president.'

2.06pm/ 3.06pm EST

Clint Hill realises to his horror what's about to happen – Mrs Kennedy will hear rifle fire for the first time since Dealey Plaza. Hill is about to walk across when John Metzler leans over and warns her. A squad from the Old Guard Regiment fire three quick volleys. Jackie flinches each time.

It is now the time for Sergeant Keith Clark to play 'The Day Is Done' on his bugle – the traditional ending to a military funeral. Clark believes he should play only for the widow, so he turns his bugle towards Mrs Kennedy. As he begins, he thinks of the words from the Bible: '...we shall all be changed, in a moment, in the twinkling of an eye, at the last trumpet: for the trumpet shall sound, and the dead shall be raised incorruptible, and we shall be changed.'

He cracks one note, but it simply sounds as if emotion got to the young bugler.

The flag from the casket is folded into a thick, neat triangle by the white-gloved hands of the honour guard, and then passed down to Private Douglas Mayfield, who hands it to the Arlington's superintendent John Metzler. As he salutes, the television audience can see that Mayfield's lips are trembling. Metzler waits for the band to finish playing 'Eternal Father Strong to Save', and then hands the flag to Jackie.

'Mrs Kennedy, this flag is presented to you in the name of a most mournful nation. Please accept it.'

2.15pm/3.15pm EST

In the pockets of Ted and Robert Kennedy are typed-out quotations from their dead brother's speeches that they planned to read during the ceremony, but what seemed a good idea in the White House doesn't feel right at the graveside. When the cardinal asks them to step forward they shake their heads.

Jackie is handed a large burning taper, and still clutching the folded flag, stoops to light the eternal flame. It leaps up at once. She then passes the taper to Robert and Ted, who symbolically light the flame. President Johnson was then supposed to do the same, but he's too far away and surrounded by bodyguards.

2.32pm/3.32pm EST

The president's casket is lowered into the grave.

2.34pm/3.34pm EST

Superintendent John Metzler knows that the only way that his staff can finish the burial in private is by taking drastic action. He orders his electrician to cut the power to the television cameras.

2.45pm/3.45pm EST

The hearse carrying JD Tippit's casket is making its way through the streets of Fort Worth to the Laurel Land Memorial Park, escorted by a 15-man motorcycle escort.

John Metzler is surprised to see that four members of the Special Forces have appeared to stand guard at each corner of the president's grave. Two years earlier, the president had revoked the order banning them wearing their green berets. When they finally leave a few hours later, one of the soldiers salutes, takes off his beret and lays it by the eternal flame. 'He gave us the beret and we thought it fitting to give one back to him,' he explains.

3.00pm

Richard Stolley of *Life* magazine is once again negotiating with Abraham Zapruder, this time in the offices of the dressmaker's lawyer Sam Passman. *Life* wants the film rights to the footage. With Passman present it makes their negotiations more formal. Once again rival journalists are camped outside, waiting to pounce should the negotiations break down. Stolley starts at $25,000.

3.10pm

In 1962, an area of Laurel Land Memorial Park in Fort Worth was designated a 'Memorial Court of Honour', a place where those who have given their lives for the community are buried. Officer JD Tippit will be the first to be laid to rest there. His casket, covered in three dozen red roses, lies by the open grave. A squad of policemen stands to attention, while seated under a green awning with her three children, his widow Marie weeps.

3.30pm

Richard Stolley has excused himself from the negotiations, saying he needs to call New York to see if they can raise their offer. In fact, he calls the Dallas operator for a weather report instead, as he knows exactly what *Life* is prepared to pay.

3.45pm

On the outskirts of Fort Worth, two unmarked Secret Service cars are on their way to Rose Hill Cemetery. Inside the first are Marguerite, Marina and her children; in the second, Robert. He stares gloomily out of the window, depressed by the attitude of the ministers and cemetery officials who've shown the Oswald family little compassion.

'What about that car behind us?' the driver says, breaking the silence. Bob Parsons, a policeman travelling with them, turns round.

'It's just two old ladies. But one of them has a burp [submachine] gun.' They all laugh, and Robert appreciates Parsons' attempt to cheer him up.

4.00pm

No one from the Oswald family has yet turned up at the chapel at Rose Hill, and the funeral is due to start. However, there are about a dozen reporters seated at the back of the chapel. Undertaker Drudie Miller comes to the front and asks the reporters if they'd carry Lee Harvey Oswald's coffin to the graveside. The pressmen look at each other. Mike Cochran of AP (who has been covering the story since the Fort Worth breakfast on Friday morning) shakes his head, but then sees Preston McGraw of rival UPI heading to the coffin, so he changes his mind and grabs a corner. In all, six newsmen volunteer. To them it's clear, if they want to write a story about the funeral of the president's assassin, they're going to have to bury him themselves.

Stolley and Zapruder agree on $150,000 for all rights to the film, to be paid in six annual instalments of $25,000. Then

Sam Passman brings up a delicate subject. He's afraid that anti-Jewish feeling in Dallas will be inflamed when people find out that his client has made money from the film. He suggests that the first $25,000 goes to Officer Tippit's widow. Stolley thinks this is an inspired suggestion and Zapruder agrees without a moment's thought.

In the staff library at Parkland Hospital, the chaplain Kenneth Pepper is preaching a sermon at a memorial service.

'Over the din of a multitude of cheering voices rang out three shots which cut down our president and seriously wounded our Governor. Neither the skill nor wisdom of the medical team, nor the resources of the richest nation on earth, nor the hopes and prayers of our souls was able to hold back the reality that the assassin's bullet had found its mark.

'Today we mourn his passing. We remember his concern for civil liberties and his concern for the underprivileged. Many have watched his work and seen in him the work of an emancipator. Many of us were critical of his methods or ideas, but all of us have been sharpened by the encounter with his life and leadership.'

4.10pm

The two cars carrying the Oswald family are at the cemetery's main gate, being searched by the Fort Worth police. As they are waved through, Robert watches people staring at them through the fence

They walk into the chapel – it's completely empty.

Eddie Hughes, a photographer for the *Dallas Morning News*, is holding onto Lee Harvey Oswald's wooden coffin and he's shocked at how heavy it is. Hughes is also feeling uneasy. His paper is very conservative and may take a dim view of one of its staff carrying an assassin's coffin. One of the other last-minute pall-bearers says, 'You realise we're making history', and Hughes starts to feel better about what he's doing.

4.12pm

'We were a few minutes late,' an agent is explaining to Robert Oswald. 'There's been some misunderstanding, and they've already carried the casket down to the grave site. We'll have a service down there.'

Robert explodes with rage and disappointment, and he hits the chapel wall with his fist.

'Damn it!' he shouts.

As they drive down the hill, Robert can see Paul Groody, the funeral director, and standing behind a rope, a large group of reporters. As they pull up, one of the Secret Service agents says to the policeman in the car, 'You stay in here with the carbine. If anything happens, come out shooting.'

'Nothing would give me greater pleasure than to mow down 15 or 20 reporters,' he replies.

Groody introduces Robert to the superintendent of Rose Hill and explains that he agreed without hesitation to sell the plot to the family. Groody suggests that, as the superintendent's job is at risk because of what he did, Robert could give the impression from now on that the plot had been owned by the Oswalds for some time. Robert is touched by the superintendent's compassion and readily agrees.

There's no sign of Reverend French, but Reverend Louis Sanders of the Disciple of Christ Church, who turned up to see if there was anything he could do to help the Oswalds, has agreed to stand in. He's a bit rusty when it comes to funerals, not having done one for eight years.

4.20pm

Marguerite, Robert and Marina are seated on aluminium chairs under the green canopy that covers the grave. Marina has Rachel on her lap, Marguerite has June. Marguerite is annoyed at the reporters, photographers, Secret Service agents and police standing around them.

'Privacy at the grave, privacy at the grave,' she pleads.

A French reporter comes over and starts speaking to Marina. Robert gets up to shoo him away, but Marina stops him.

'He... says... sorrow.'

Robert asks agent Mike Howard to move all the bystanders back, as he'd like the coffin opened so that he can see his brother, having been denied the chance at Parkland. Once the agents have lined up to form a protective screen, Paul Groody opens the lid. The family walks to the coffin. Lee is dressed in a dark brown suit, brown tie and white shirt. Marina kisses him, then puts two rings on one of his fingers. Robert takes a long, last look at his brother.

4.30pm/5.30pm EST

Two cars are driving down Main Street in Dallas, each carrying a placard saying, 'In Memory of our beloved President. God Bless Jack Ruby.'

At a reception at the White House for the foreign dignitaries and heads of state, Jackie opens a door and finds Prince Philip sitting on the floor playing with John Jr. Philip blushes, and says how much John Jr reminds him of Prince Charles at that age.

'John, did you make your bow to the prince?' Jackie asks.

'I did!' John Jr replies, triumphantly, and they all laugh. As she walks away, Jackie remembers how when flying to London on her first trip there as first lady, she'd called the chief of protocol, Angier Duke, to the back of Air Force One to ask whether she should curtsey to the queen. Duke had replied that the wife of the chief of state never curtsies for anyone.

Jackie realises that she had just curtsied to Prince Philip.

'Angie, I'm no longer the wife of a chief of state...' she says to Duke when she sees him a few moments later.

At Rose Hill, Reverend Saunders is searching for the right words to say at a burial that is unlike any other he has presided over.

'We are not here to stand in judgement of him. We are here only to lay him to rest. God of the open sky and infinite universe, we pray and petition for this family who are heart-broken. Those who suffer and who have tears in their hearts will pray for them... their need is great.'

He looks at the coffin.

'May God have mercy on his soul.'

4.40pm/5.40pm EST

Marguerite and Marina and the children are walking back to the car. Robert is hesitating by the grave.

'Would you like to stay until your brother's body is lowered?' a Secret Service agent asks him.

'Yes, for a few minutes.'

So Robert watches as Paul Groody's men slowly lower the coffin, now in a concrete casket, into the grave. The words inscribed on the top, 'Lee Harvey Oswald 1939 – 1963', disappear from sight.

At the White House reception, Jackie is talking to a visibly moved Anastas Mikoyan.

'My husband's dead. Now peace is up to you,' Jackie says.

A few days later she would write to President Khrushchev: 'I tried to give him a message to you that day – but as it was such a terrible day for me, I do not know if my words came out as I meant them to.'

6.00pm/7.00pm EST

In the Kennedy family quarters of the White House, a birthday party for three-year-old John is taking place. He and Caroline are seated at a small table, surrounded by cousins and uncles and aunts. John Jr is opening a large pile of presents, and waiting for him is a cake with candles. Maud Shaw is busy supervising proceedings. Dave Powers leads the group in singing 'Happy Birthday'.

Jackie suggests they sing some more songs, and so Powers and Ted and Robert Kennedy start singing 'Heart of My Heart', a favourite of JFK. The words fill the second floor of the White House. As he sings, Robert remembers when he, Ted and Jack had climbed onto a table in a Boston deli at the end of the 1958 Massachusetts senatorial campaign, and had sung it in front of an enthusiastic crowd. It's almost too much for him.

Dave Powers tells stories of his time with Jack – how he first met him when Jack knocked on the door of his third-floor Boston tenement flat and said, 'My name is Jack Kennedy. I'm a candidate for Congress. Will you help me...?' And how he had said later, 'If I had gotten tired that night when I reached the second floor, I would never have met you.'

10.55pm/ 11.55pm EST

Clint Hill is walking behind Jackie and Robert Kennedy up the slope towards JFK's grave. Earlier, as the guests had headed for home, Robert had said to Jackie, 'Shall we go visit our friend?'

Arlington Cemetery is dark and quiet, and when they get to the grave they can see that it's changed in only a few hours. A white picket fence has been placed around the plot, and people have leant hundreds of flowers against it. Robert Kennedy notices the Special Forces beret and other military caps that have joined it around the eternal flame. Clint Hill watches as Jackie, illuminated by the light of the flame, places her posy of lily of the valley on the ground.

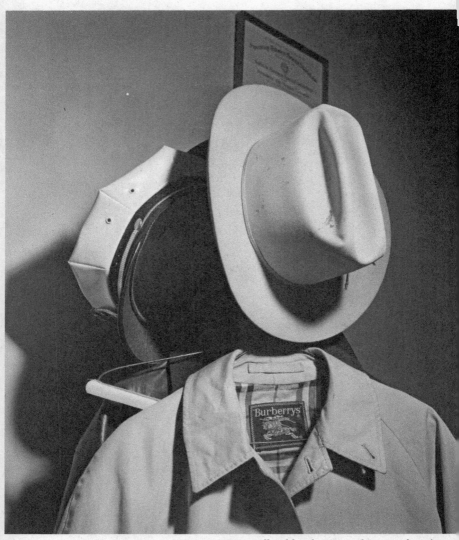

*Governor Connally's blood-spattered Stetson hanging
in Chief Curry's office.*

After November 1963...

Jackie Kennedy

Jackie plunged herself into shaping her husband's legacy, for example allowing Idlewild to be renamed John F Kennedy International Airport, and deciding that the John F Kennedy Presidential Library and Museum should be the only national memorial to her husband. Although their marriage wasn't perfect (she knew of JFK's womanising) it was Jackie who, within a week of the assassination, compared the end of the Kennedy White House to the end of Camelot. In October 1968 she married Aristotle Onassis. Jackie died of cancer in May 1994 and was buried next to JFK at Arlington.

Caroline Kennedy

Jackie moved her family to New York, where they spent their childhood. Caroline went on to study at Harvard and Columbia Law School, and publish books on constitutional law. She carries on her mother's work of keeping her father's name alive – she is president of the Kennedy Library Foundation and helped found the Profile in Courage Award, named after JFK's 1956 book *Profiles in Courage*. Caroline is married with two girls, Rose and Tatiana, and a son, John, named after her father.

John Jr

After JFK's assassination, his children continued to fascinate the world's press. A few weeks after the assassination, a newspaper photographer took John Jr's picture in a park. 'What are you taking my picture for?' he said, 'My Daddy's dead.' John went on to follow his sister into law and served for four years as a prosecutor in Manhattan's district attorney's office. On 16th July 1999, John Jr, his wife and sister-in-law were killed when the light plane he was piloting crashed into the sea off Martha's Vineyard.

Robert Kennedy

Robert continued to serve as attorney general for another nine months and then left Johnson's Cabinet to run successfully for senator of New York. On 16th March 1968 he announced his candidacy for president in the same room where JFK had, at the same age, eight years earlier. On 6th June, having just won the California Primary, Robert Kennedy was shot dead, aged only 42. He too was buried at Arlington Cemetery.

Lyndon B Johnson

Within months of the assassination in Dallas, Johnson skilfully managed to get two key pieces of JFK legislation enacted – a tax cut and a new civil rights bill. In 1964 he was elected president with the widest popular margin in American history. He served only one term, and died of a heart attack at his Texas ranch in January 1973.

Clint Hill

In December 1963, Jackie Kennedy presented Clint Hill (and Rufus Youngblood who had dived on top of Lyndon Johnson when the shooting started) with an award for bravery. Hill protected her for another year. He retired from the Secret Service in 1975. Hill was plagued by drink problems and nightmares about the assassination, and continued to feel guilty that he could have saved the president if he'd been standing on the back of the car. Then, in 1990, Hill visited the sixth floor of the Book Depository for the first time. Looking out of the window, he could see that Oswald had a perfect line of sight and agents on the back of the Lincoln would have made little difference. He left convinced that he had done the best he could that day.

Bob Foster

Jackie Kennedy requested that Bob Foster continue to protect Caroline and John Jr, which he did until they moved to New York in the summer of 1964. When Foster retired in September 1978, Jackie wrote to him, 'I shall always remember the happy days Caroline and John spent with you, and the Secret Service has been most fortunate in having such a dedicated and devoted agent on the force all these years.' Bob Foster died in 2008, aged 78.

Kenny O'Donnell

O'Donnell served as an aide for Lyndon Johnson until January 1965. For the rest of his life he believed that because he was responsible for the itinerary of the trip to Texas, he was partly to blame for the president's death. The murder in 1968 of his best friend Robert Kennedy hastened his descent into alcoholism. Kenny O'Donnell died in 1977. In 2000, Kevin Costner played him in the Cuban Missile Crisis movie *Thirteen Days*.

Dave Powers

In the months after the assassination, Dave Powers (suffering from headaches at the back of the head, exactly where the second bullet hit JFK) came faithfully every day to play with John Jr and Caroline. When Kenny O'Donnell offered his resignation to Johnson, the president said, 'When you leave take Dave Powers with you. He's never worked for anybody around here except you and the Kennedys anyway.' Powers became the first curator of the John F Kennedy Library in Boston, a post he held until he retired in 1994. He died four years later.

Marina Oswald

In 1965 Marina married drag racer Kenneth Jess Porter with whom she had two sons. For many years she worked as a shop assistant in a Dallas store. Although she was initially convinced that Lee was guilty of assassinating Kennedy, Marina now believes he was completely innocent, and that a KGB agent impersonating her husband shot JFK. In 1981, persuaded by conspiracy theorists that it was the Soviet agent she buried and not Lee, she allowed a team of scientists to exhume the body. Robert Oswald vehemently opposed the exhumation. Tests proved that the body was that of Lee Harvey Oswald. Marina still lives in Dallas and continues to believe in her husband's innocence.

Robert Oswald

Until his death in November 2017, Robert maintained that his brother killed President Kennedy and that he acted alone.

Marguerite Oswald

Within a few days of her son's death, Marguerite was selling his letters and school reports to the highest bidder. She kept her number listed in the Fort Worth telephone directory, always willing to talk to journalists for money. Marguerite died of cancer in 1982, convinced that Lee had been employed by the CIA to assassinate President Kennedy as a 'mercy killing' because he was terminally ill. For reasons best known to herself, Marguerite had a plaque made for her house, 'My son, Lee Harvey Oswald, even after his death has done more for his country than any other living human being.'

Jack Ruby

Following JFK's assassination and Oswald's murder, Ruby's mental state deteriorated considerably, perhaps indicating that he may have been in the early stages of mental illness by November 1963. Ruby became convinced that American Jews were being slaughtered because of his crime, and that he could hear his brother Sam being tortured outside the jail. Ruby tried to kill himself three times.

In March 1964, he was convicted of committing murder with malice and sentenced to death. His lawyers appealed, saying that a fair trial had been impossible in Dallas. They won, and a new trial was set for February 1967, but by then Ruby had been diagnosed with cancer. He died on 3rd January 1967, in the same hospital as JFK and Oswald, the Parkland. His autopsy was carried out by the man who did everything by the book, Earl Rose.

Maud Shaw

Miss Shaw retired in 1965 and came home to England to live in Sheerness with her brother and sister, and that same year published *White House Nannie*, a memoir of her seven years with the Kennedy family.

Ruth Paine

Ruth Paine and Marina never saw each other again after November 1963. Ruth spent much of her life as a teacher and school principal and is now retired. Her former home at 2515 Fifth Street is being turned into a museum by the city of Irving. Ruth said in 2003, 'My sense of loss of President Kennedy, my sense of regret at having known the assassin, those just stay with me.'

Jesse Curry

For many years Curry received hate mail accusing him of complicity in Oswald's murder. His handling of events after JFK's assassination damaged his reputation and he resigned as police chief in March 1966. In a book published three years later, he suggested that there could have been a gunman on the grassy knoll, who fired the final shot that killed Kennedy. Jesse Curry died of a heart attack in 1980.

Captain Will Fritz

Fritz never spoke publicly about the events of November 1963. He retired from the police service in 1970 and died 14 years later, aged 89.

Henry Wade

In 1970, Wade's office defended Texas abortion laws in the famous Roe versus Wade case. It led to the landmark 1973 Supreme Court ruling that made abortion legal in the United States. It's said it was the only case that Henry Wade ever lost. He died in 2001.

John and Nellie Connally

John Connally went on to serve two more terms as governor. In 1971 he became President Nixon's treasury secretary and switched to the Republican Party shortly after. He died in 1993 of pulmonary fibrosis, a disease that involves scarring of the lungs. His wife Nellie is convinced that it was caused by the damage done by the slivers of bone that were shattered by Oswald's bullet.

Bibliography

Aynesworth, Hugh, *JFK: Breaking the News* (IFP, 2003)

Benson, Michael, *Who's Who In the JFK Assassination* (Citadel Press, 1993)

Bishop, Jim, *The Day Kennedy Was Shot* (Harper Perennial, 1992)

Blaine, Gerald, *The Kennedy Detail* (Gallery Books, 2010)

Bugliosi, Vincent, *Four Days In November* (W.W. Norton, 2007)

Caro, Robert A, *The Years of Lyndon Johnson Volume 4: The Passage of Power* (The Bodley Head, 2012)

Clarke, Nick, *Alistair Cooke The Biography* (Weidenfeld & Nicolson, 1999)

Connally, Nellie, *From Love Field* (Rugged Land, 2003)

Cooke, Alistair, *Reporting America* (Allen Lane, 2008)

Dallek, Robert, *John F Kennedy An Unfinished Life* (Penguin, 2003)

Grosvenor, Melville Bell, *The Last Full Measure* (National Geographic, 1964)

Hamilton, Nigel, *JFK: The Life and Death of an American President* (BCA, 1992)

Heyman, C David, *Bobby and Jackie* (Atria Books, 2009)

Hill, Clint, *Mrs Kennedy and Me* (Gallery Books, 2012)

Hlavach, Laura and Payne, Darwin, *Reporting the Kennedy Assassination* (Three Forks Press, 1996)

Hosty, James P Jr, *Assignment: Oswald* (Arcade Publishing, 1996)

Huffaker, Bob, Mercer, Bil, Phoenix, George and Wise, Wes, *When The News went Live: Dallas 1963* (Taylor Trade Publishing, 2004)

MacNeil, Robert, *The Right Place at the Right Time* (Penguin, 1982)

Manchester, William, *The Death of a President* (World Books, 1967)

McMillan, Priscilla Johnson, *Marina and Lee* (Harper & Row, 1977)

Miall, Leonard, *Richard Dimbleby Broadcaster* (BBC, 1966)

O'Donnell, Helen, *A Common Good* (William Murrow and Co, 1998)

O'Donnell, Kenneth P and Powers, David F, *Johnny, We Hardly Knew Ye* (Little, Brown, 1970)

Oswald, Robert, *Lee: A Portrait of Lee Harvey Oswald* (Coward-McCann, 1967)

Peel, John and Ravenscroft, Sheila, *Margrave of the Marshes* (Bantam Press, 2005)

Posner, Gerald, *Case Closed* (Anchor Books, 1993)

Schlesinger, Arthur M Jr, *Robert Kennedy and His Times* (Ballantine Books, 1978)

Semple, Robert B Jr ed, *Four Days in November* (St Martin's Press, 2003)

Shaw, Maud, *White House Nannie* (The New American Library, 1965)

Sherrin, Ned, *The Autobiography* (Little, Brown, 2005)

West, JB, *Upstairs at the White House* (Warner Paperback, 1973)

Wills, Garry and Demaris, Ovid, *Jack Ruby* (Da Capo Press, 1994)

Other Sources

Stolley, Richard B, "What Happened Next", *Esquire*, November 1973

JFK: Breaking the News, KERA Dallas

Kennedy's Cadets, Nemeton TV

On This Day/Witness, bbc.co.uk

The Warren Commission Report and Exhibits

Acknowledgements

The *Minute by Minute* concept began life as a live Radio 2 programme by TBI Media to mark the centenary of the sinking of the *Titanic*. The idea wouldn't have got off the ground without the help and considerable skill and support of Phil Critchlow, the director of TBI – one of the good guys. My thanks also to his team at Great Titchfield Street.

I owe a debt of gratitude to Bob Shennan, the controller of Radio 2, and to Robert Gallagher, its commissioning editor, for seeing the potential of the *Minute by Minute* idea and supporting it all the way.

Rebecca Nicolson, Aurea Carpenter, Paul Bougourd and Emma Craigie at the mighty Short Books believed *Minute by Minute* could work in book form and have steered this novice through the publishing process with great patience.

Bruce Cowie of the Black Watch Regiment, Nicholas Herbert of *The Times* and Barry Heads of Granada TV were kind enough to let me grill them about their memories of November 1963. The late Sir Denis Forman gave me an invaluable steer a few months before he died. Mark Davies of the Sixth Floor Museum at Dealey Plaza helped source stills from their remarkable collection. Thank you all.

Finally, thanks to my mother, and to my father who passed on to me a passion for history – he'd have loved this book. Love and thanks to Charlie who seems to have caught the history bug, and to Hannah for her suggestions, love and support.

Index